Down to the River and Up to the Trees

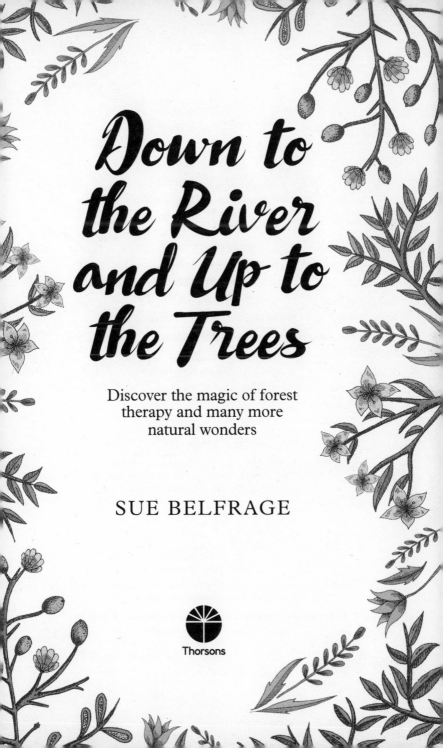

Down to the River and Up to the Trees

Discover the magic of forest
therapy and many more
natural wonders

SUE BELFRAGE

Thorsons

Thorsons
An imprint of HarperCollins*Publishers*
1 London Bridge Street
London SE1 9GF

www.harpercollins.co.uk

First published by HarperCollins*Publishers* 2017
This edition published 2018

1 3 5 7 9 10 8 6 4 2

Text and illustrations © Sue Belfrage 2017

The poem 'Night Blanket' first published in *Mslexia* magazine in 2016

Sue Belfrage asserts the moral right to be
identified as the author of this work

A catalogue record of this book is
available from the British Library

ISBN 978-0-00-831368-5

Printed and bound by CPI Group (UK) Ltd, Croydon

MIX
Paper from
responsible sources
FSC™ C007454

This book is produced from independently certified FSC™ paper
to ensure responsible forest management.

For more information visit: www.harpercollins.co.uk/green

—— ∞ ——

To see a World in a Grain of Sand
And a Heaven in a Wild Flower,
Hold Infinity in the palm of your hand
And Eternity in an hour.

WILLIAM BLAKE (1757–1827), 'Auguries of Innocence'

To Matt, man of the woods

Contents

— Water —

— Wood —

— Feather —

— Fur —

Introduction

First, a confession – I've never been to the Serengeti
to marvel at lions. Nor have I witnessed a sunset in the
Australian outback, or swum with brilliantly coloured fish
over a coral reef. Yet I still remember one of the first times I
saw a creature in the wild that made me gasp out loud.

I was sitting on the back of a motorbike at the time, riding
pillion at 65 mph. And the creature that caught my eye was
a buzzard, waddling across a field by the side of the road.
It wasn't soaring, swooping or doing anything particularly
impressive. Most probably it was grubbing about for worms.
But I was left buzzing at the thought that such a large bird
of prey could exist, free to wander where it liked, within a
couple of hours' drive from London.

Today I live in the countryside and am surrounded by
footpaths, green fields and woodland. And each time I step
outside I'm struck again by the amazing variety of life –
animals, insects, fungi and plants – that surrounds us.

But you don't have to live in the countryside to experience
that sense of wonder. Wherever your home and wherever you
find yourself – suburb or seaside, tower block or terrace –
you too are surrounded by living, breathing, growing beings,
be they trees, bees or woodlice.

All the suggestions in this book are designed to help you
create your own sense of connection with the natural world.
If you're drawn to this idea, you probably know intuitively
that spending time in nature can be good for us. There's a

growing body of scientific evidence in support of nature's many health benefits, from helping us destress and find calm, to strengthening the immune system and fighting disease, improving memory and creativity, and grounding ourselves in the present moment.

Most of the activities can be enjoyed at any time of year, although a few, such as nutting, are dependent on the seasons. Throughout this journal you'll find plenty of inspirational quotes from great nature writers, and you're invited to add to these by jotting down your own thoughts, ideas, sketches and observations. There's also a section of Notes (see page 183), left blank especially for you to use. Please don't worry about marking any of the pages, crossing out stuff or making a mess; use this book in the way that works best for you, perhaps as a departure point, or as a storehouse in which to gather together your experiences, just like a squirrel stashes acorns in autumn.

Other than being mindful of safety – for instance, when handling sharp tools – there are no firm rules. Be kind and give yourself permission to try things out, adapting them in whatever way suits you. Follow your instincts. Some of the ideas might be a better fit for you than others, or need a bit of adapting depending on the circumstances; nobody is going to judge you on the results.

When you do venture out and about in the natural world, please keep your wits about you and respect the environment. Be mindful that, as the poet Tennyson said, nature can be 'red in tooth and claw'. If you go walking and don't want to get lost, take a map (and keep a wary eye out for cows – more people are killed by cattle in the UK than tigers, that's for sure). If you want to try wild swimming, check that you can get out of the water as easily as you can hop in. While some of the suggestions in this book might seem a little like child's play, the intention isn't to treat nature like a recreation ground, without any thought for other animals, plants and people; it's about rediscovering the playful sense of curiosity and calm wonder that spending time in nature can nurture.

This journal isn't a spotter's guide and won't, for example, tell you the weight of a robin's egg or give you the Latin name of the common frog. If, however, your curiosity is piqued, perhaps you'll go on to do a bit of research of your own. As mentioned, the Notes section at the back is designed to provide a useful space in which to record your findings, whatever shape they take. And who knows what that might be – scientific insights, lines of poetry or quick sketches of things that catch your eye?

This much I can tell you: there's a whole beautiful wild world out there, right on your doorstep, just waiting to be discovered. And it's time to make yourself truly at home in it.

Earth

he Earth is our home in the solar system, and the soil beneath our feet. If you ever feel disconnected from your surroundings, go outside and stand barefoot for a moment or two, take a couple of deep breaths and focus on the uneven surface under your soles and toes. If you'd prefer to ground yourself by getting your hands dirty, try foraging for wild foods or consider growing your own. Perhaps build a wormery. Or walk somewhere new that leads you into the past.

Create a sense of rootedness and belonging wherever you find yourself by familiarising yourself with the smells, sights and tastes that surround you. Discover the plants that thrive against the odds and hidden wildlife.

Welcome yourself back to where you belong.

—— ∞ ——

'Live in each season as it passes; breathe the air, drink the drink, taste the fruit, and resign yourself to the influence of the earth.'

HENRY DAVID THOREAU (1817–1862), *Walden*

Being Here

Choose a place that you can visit easily. It could be your garden or balcony, an allotment or stretch of hedgerow, perhaps a park bench or even the corner of a car park. Somewhere you can go and sit or stand without being disturbed for a few minutes; turning off your phone will help. Don't worry about being stared at; most people are too busy with their own stuff to notice if you sit quietly. (Of course, if you do want others to give you a wide berth, you could try singing the national anthem at the top of your voice; that should work.)

Mark out an area that's about 1 metre, or an arm span, square. Think of it as a pillar that stretches from the ground up into the sky. Now focus.

* What can you see?
* What do you hear, smell or sense?
* Is there anything in particular that delights you?
* Or is there anything that disgusts you?
* How does the air feel on your skin, on your face, ears and hands?
* Can you hear bird calls or the sounds of animals?
* What insects are crawling or flying around you?
* What other creatures might have passed this way?
* What difference do you make, being here now?
* And what difference might you make, without disturbing the habitat of any creatures that live

here? Could you tend to the plot in some way, perhaps by clearing away litter?

∗ Repeat to yourself: 'I belong here.'
∗ You are part of it all.

If you like, why not return here once a day or once a week for a month? Make a note of your changing observations as time passes.

—— ∞ ——

'Come forth into the light of things,
Let Nature be your teacher.'

William Wordsworth (1770–1850), 'The Tables Turned'

A Map of Smells

If you're ever out and about, and come across a spot used by a fox to scent-mark its territory, you'll find the odour hard to ignore: so strong and musky, it can often be smelt even if you're driving past in a car with the windows shut.

There's a particular corner in the middle of the village where I live that always smells of fox. Mind you, the village as a whole often smells of muck-spreading and cows, so there are probably people who crinkle their noses at the entire place as they drive past. I guess I don't notice the whiff as much as visitors do; it's just what I'm used to. But I don't think we should underestimate the power of smell when it comes to making sense of our surroundings, or how important smell is in stoking our impressions and memories of a place.

Here's a suggestion. On a warm day, when scents are likely to be strong, or after a shower of rain, why not tune into your sense of smell and make an olfactory map? You can do this either on foot, scribbling down notes as you go, or, if travelling by some other means, maybe on a sketch when you get home. What strikes you? Which smells are familiar and which are unexpected? Pungent or pleasing? Plant, animal or mineral?

Once you have tuned into your sense of smell, you might be surprised by just how much you pick up, and how important those smells are in shaping your relationship with a place.

Good Enough to Eat

Few things taste as delicious as blackberries picked straight from the hedgerow or an apple plucked from the tree. Likewise, it can be hugely rewarding to grow your own food or forage for your dinner.

If you do decide to go foraging, please make sure you have expert advice about whatever it is that you choose to gather. The consequences of eating that tasty-looking mushroom (which turns out to be poisonous) or the pip of a plump yew berry, for instance, are just too dire to contemplate.

Whether or not you do go and pick your own, it's good to be aware of that sense of disconnection that can sometimes exist between the food on our plates and its origins in nature. Next time you have a meal, why not try the following:

* Take a good look at the food in front of you. What are the basic ingredients?
* What plants and/or animals did those ingredients come from?
* Can you make a conscious connection between your meal and the various elements in it – animal, mineral and vegetable?
* In what ways might those elements be nourishing you? How might they be feeding the ways in which you see the world, as well as the cells in your body?

Wild Rosehip Soup

Nyponsoppa, or rosehip soup, is a traditional Scandinavian favourite that I used to enjoy as a child when we lived in Sweden for a few years. It's made from the bright orangey-red fruit of the dog rose (*Rosa canina*), which grows wild in hedgerows. The soup is served as a snack, or as a dessert with almond biscuits on the side.

While you can make the soup from freshly picked rosehips, it's much more usual to make it from dried hips. Pick your own in the autumn and dry them slowly for a few hours on a tray in the oven on a very low heat. (You can see why the Aga was invented in Sweden.) When you've taken the dried rosehips out of the oven, let them cool and store them in an airtight container somewhere dry. If stored well, they should last a couple of years – so it's worth getting your supplies in.

Serves 4

500 g (1 lb 1 oz) dried, whole wild rosehips
1½ litres (50 fl oz) water
150 g (5 oz) sugar
1½ tbsp potato flour (or cornflour)
Double/whipped cream, to serve

When you're ready to make your soup, soak the dried
rosehips in half of the water for a few hours or overnight.
Then cook them in the same water, over a medium heat in a
large saucepan, until they are soft and sticky, which should
take about 25 minutes.

Blend the rosehip mixture with a stick blender or in a mixer,
then strain through a fine sieve and return the liquid to the
saucepan. Add the rest of the water and stir in the sugar. Mix
up the potato flour or cornflour with a little water and pour
the mixture steadily into the soup, stirring it in.

Cook until the soup thickens, then remove the saucepan
from the heat and allow to cool a little. Ladle the lukewarm
soup into bowls and swirl through a little double cream or
add a dollop of whipped cream before serving.

Hedgerow Jam

What could be nicer than homemade jam on hot toast? What's more, blackberries can be picked for free from hedgerows and thickets throughout the summer. To make about six jars of your own blackberry jam you will need:

> 1.5 kg (3 lb 5 oz) blackberries
> 4 tbsp water
> Juice of 1 lemon
> 1.5 kg (3 lb 5 oz) sugar
> Tiny knob of butter (optional)

Wash the blackberries and put them in a large pan with the water and lemon juice. Simmer gently over a low heat until the fruit turns squishy. Add the sugar and heat gradually. While you are heating the mixture, put a saucer in the fridge to chill.

Once the sugar has dissolved, bring the jam to the boil for about 10 minutes, stirring constantly. To test whether your jam will set, plop a teaspoonful on the cold saucer and poke the edge of the jam. If the surface wrinkles, it will set.

When the jam's ready, remove the saucepan from the heat and skim the foam from the top. To dissolve any remaining foam, stir a tiny knob of butter the size of a fingernail into the froth and remove with a spoon. Allow the jam to cool

and thicken for about 10 minutes before pouring carefully
into sterilised jam jars and sealing straightaway.

Tradition has it that the devil was thrown out of heaven on
29 September, Michaelmas Day, and landed on a blackberry
bush. He promptly peed on the berries in revenge, which is
why it's best to pick them before October.

Mushroom Mayhem

As a child I used to go mushroom picking with neighbours and return home with baskets full of chanterelles and ceps. These days, however, I'm more cautious. While mushroom foraging is a lovely thing to do, it can occasionally go very wrong. If it appeals to you, please consult a reliable field guide or go picking with somebody who knows what they're talking about. Or you could try growing your own.

For those with limited space there are mushroom windowsill kits. You can make your own version by sprinkling some grain spawn for oyster mushrooms onto the soaked pages of an old catalogue or paperback. Once you've done this, wrap the catalogue in a plastic bag. Punch small holes in the bag and leave the package somewhere dark and warm for a few weeks, keeping the contents moist but not dripping wet. (If the package turns black, it's gone mouldy and is no good.) When a white furry layer of mycelium appears over the catalogue, place the package in the fridge for a day or two to shock the mycelium into action. Then store the package in a cool spot such as under the sink or in a cellar. If all goes to plan, over the next few days tiny mushrooms should start to sprout. Let them grow until they look big enough to eat.

If you've more room and patience, you can plant mushroom dowels impregnated with spores in holes drilled in a hardwood log, then seal them over with beeswax. This process can take over a year to yield results, but it could be the gift that keeps on giving.

Grow Your Own

It's fairly easy to grow your own vegetables wherever you live. To grow your own potatoes, any sturdy container will do. You could, for instance, use an empty dumpy bag, folding down the sides so the bag is about 40 cm (16 in) deep, or use an old compost bag or burlap sack.

For drainage, pierce a couple of small holes in the bag and add a layer of sand or other drainage material such as broken crockery or pebbles at the bottom. Then cover this layer with about 10 cm (4 in) of soil and compost mix.

How many seed potatoes you plant will depend on the size of your container, as they shouldn't be crammed in. For a 40 litre (8.5 gallon) container, plant just three seed potatoes. Then cover these with enough soil–compost mix to keep them hidden.

Position the bag in a sunny spot and keep the soil moist. As the plants grow and shoots come up, carry on covering these with the soil–compost mix. That way, your plants will send out more roots – giving you more potatoes. When the soil level reaches the top of the bag, let the plants flower and die. Now it's time to dig around in the soil for your crop. Depending on the type of seed potatoes you use, it may take around 90 days to get to this stage, but it's well worth the wait.

Worm Wizardry

My friend Bill has fallen in love with his pet worms. They live in a wormery in his shed, are no bother and eat up leftovers. To make your own wormery and create compost for flowerbeds or plant pots you will need:

* A large plastic or wooden box with a lid, approximately 46 cm wide by 35 cm high (18 × 14 in).
* A drill with a 12 mm (½ in) drill bit.
* Bricks or blocks to stand the wormery on.
* A tray or bucket.
* A couple of sheets of newspaper and a piece of cardboard.
* Worm bedding such as old compost or coir.
* 300–400 composting worms such as tiger, brandling, manure or red worms, available online and from fishing tackle shops or manure heaps (not earthworms, as these live in soil, not compost).

Drill 15–20 holes in the bottom of the box to let in enough air for the worms and to allow any liquid to drain out. Drill a few more air holes in the lid and at the very top of the box's sides.

Stand the box on the bricks or blocks in a sheltered spot where the wormery won't get too hot or cold. Place a tray or bucket underneath to catch any liquid, which can be used as a fertilizer when diluted with 10 parts water.

Cover the bottom of the box with a layer of newspaper or cardboard, and cover this with about 8 cm (3¼ in) of moist bedding material that the worms can burrow down into.

Introduce the worms to their new home – the good news is that you don't have to name them individually – and cover them with about 9 cm (3½ in) of kitchen waste. This can include any raw vegetables (apart from onions, garlic and leeks) and fruit (except citrus peel, which is too acidic). They're also partial to cooked vegetables, a bit of bread or pasta, tea bags and coffee grounds, egg shells, small amounts of garden greenery and a few shreds of newspaper – but not glossy magazines.

Cover the food layer with a sheet of cardboard or a damp cloth to keep the worms happy in the dark. Close the lid on the box, and leave them to settle in for about a week.

Don't overfeed your pet worms or they will start to smell. If the food layer doesn't appear to be going down, remove some of it and leave them to work their way through the rest. Feeding them little and often is best. And please don't allow the box to become waterlogged as the worms need to breathe; only add water if the wormery begins to look too dry.

It should take about eight to twelve months for the wormery to fill up. Separate out the worms before using any compost, and start the wormery again with the top 20 cm (8 in). Enjoy the many benefits of your wriggly pets.

Sounds True

Go for a walk. As you move along, tune in to your sense of hearing. What can you hear? The noise of traffic, bird song, people, dogs barking, the wind rattling, the sounds of your own movements – your breath, the rustle of your clothes?

Stop still in your tracks. What can you hear now?

Close your eyes and retune. What noises can you detect in the distance?

Keeping your eyes shut, listen in close. What else do you hear?

Experiment with shifting your focus from nearby to the distance, as if sonically scanning your surroundings.

This simple exercise can be a great way to centre yourself for a moment wherever you are.

—— ∞ ——

'The three great elemental sounds in nature are the sound of rain, the sound of wind in a primeval wood, and the sound of outer ocean on a beach.'

HENRY BESTON (1888–1968), *The Outermost House*

Litter Bug

When I take the dog for a walk, it's usually an opportunity to think and unwind. However, it can have the opposite effect when I find the track covered in rubbish. Sometimes, it looks as though somebody has had a party in their car, then chucked everything straight out of the window.

Still, there's no point complaining without doing anything about it. Although the presence of litter can act like permission for other people to start treating a place like a dump, happily it doesn't take much to reverse the trend. Everyone can make a difference by doing a bit of clearing up; what's more, it leaves you with a nice smug glow, knowing you've done your good deed for the day.

Have a go; maybe start by picking up one piece of trash a day, and – if you catch the litter-picking bug – go online and see if there are any local clean-up schemes you can take part in. You'll get to enjoy some fresh air, meet new people and leave the world a better place.

Not bad for a rubbish day out.

Hunting – With a Camera

A lot of the time we're advised to switch off phones and electronic devices if we want to find peace and calm. However, there are ways in which modern technology can be an asset when it comes to connecting with nature. I, for one, enjoy taking photos with my phone when I'm out walking, and sharing the images on social media. I've even been known to stand on mountain tops with an iPad, clicking away.

My photos aren't masterpieces by any manner of means, but pausing to take them means stopping in my tracks and taking a good look around – at the quality of light, the play of shadows, plant life, birds, animals, insects and the weather. All the same, I make sure I don't just look through a lens – that the device doesn't remain stuck in front of me like some sort of oblong obstacle – it's a back-up: first I see something beautiful or striking, then I use the camera to capture the moment, not the other way round.

You could start your own record of images of nature, printing out your favourites and sticking them here in your journal, or sharing them online. Perhaps set yourself a challenge and take a photo a day for a week or a month? Your images could be of anything: the pattern raindrops make on glass, the way lichen speckles a wall, or a stunning view. Why not stick one of your favourite photos in the frame opposite? (Or, if you prefer, stick a frame of your own over it.)

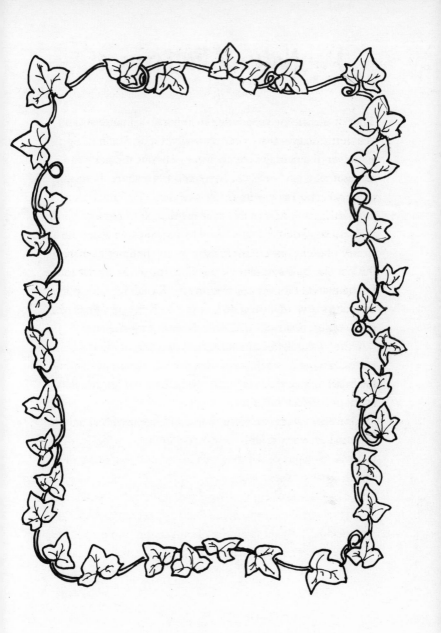

EARTH

Natural Patterns

There's something especially satisfying about patterns and geometric shapes that occur naturally. Think of the five pips arranged in a pentagon at an apple's core or the perfect hexagon of a bee's cell in a honeycomb – a shape as strong in construction as it is lovely to look at.

Another well-known example is the shell of the sea mollusc known as the nautilus, which grows in a logarithmic spiral, whereby each new chamber of its shell is bigger than the last one by a constant factor. This pattern is similar to the mathematical Fibonacci series, in which each number is the sum of the two that precede it (e.g. 1,1, 2, 3, 5, 8). Snails and many other molluscs build their shells in a similar way.

Other naturally occurring shapes and patterns include waves, lines and tessellations. Imagine the ripples of sand on the beach where the tide has recently gone out, or the sleek, overlapping scales of a fish. On a particularly freezing day, ice flowers of frost can form in fractals – geometrical patterns repeated on every scale – on window glass.

Look for signs of nature's symmetry and note down or sketch what you see.

Rock Art

One bright winter's day, I was walking along the beach when I came across some stunning rock art. Now, this beach is part of England's Jurassic Coast, famous for its fossils, but the art hadn't been created by cavemen. In fact, I don't know who made it – although I'm glad they did.

Somebody had carefully balanced huge pebbles on top of each other to create sculptures looking out to sea like a row of Easter Island heads. A single push would have toppled each of them over, yet every person on the beach that day walked round them respectfully, smiling.

The low Sun cast the sculptures' long shadows over the surrounding rocks and sand. When the tide came in, the stones would have inevitably been tumbled by the waves. So while the sculptures were monumental, they weren't intended to be permanent; yet the sight has stayed with me ever since.

The next time you find yourself in rocky surroundings, perhaps you might be inspired to create your own pebble art. You could stack your stones or arrange them in a spiral – whatever pleases you. Don't pull apart an existing stone wall or construction to source your materials; just make use of whatever you find readily to hand, in the knowledge that your creation might not last but it'll still be a work of art.

Earthworks

The countryside around where I live is dotted with ancient earthworks – from Glastonbury Tor to prehistoric hillforts that rise like slumbering dragons from the fields. Carved into the landscape, these ancient settlements and burial grounds often feel charged with a special atmosphere, as though they're indifferent to our modern comings and goings.

Of course, most towns and cities are situated on the sites of much older settlements. Even a new town such as Milton Keynes, founded in 1967, is built on land rich in Stone Age and Bronze Age archaeological finds. With a little bit of research, you too can uncover the antique roots of the place where you live.

Find out whether there are any particular landmarks in your area, or sites mentioned in old records, and visit them. Make a note of what you discover – recording the historical facts as well as the atmosphere, whether there are any clues to the place's past such as place names or particular features, and how it appears today.

Wild Grass Cord

For millennia, people have woven grass and reeds into baskets and matting. Dried grass smells sweet as a summer memory, and leisurely weaving it into cord can make for a simple yet practical keepsake.

To make the cord, pick eight or so strands of dried grass – or thin strands of creeper such as wild clematis – which are about 45 cm (18 in) long. If the material seems too dry and brittle to weave, soak it in water for about ten minutes. Then divide it into two hanks. Knot the hanks together at one end, keeping them separate. Pinch the top hank of grass between your finger and thumb and twist it tightly away from you three times with a little movement, like winding a clock; then take the bottom hank and weave this up behind the twisted hank towards you to sit at the top instead. (Like plaiting, it's much easier to do than it sounds.)

Keep repeating the process, twisting the hank on top three times, then weaving the hank underneath so that it sits at the top. If you like, thread on beads. If you run out of grass, you can splice in more until you reach the length you want. Tie a knot in the end and you're done.

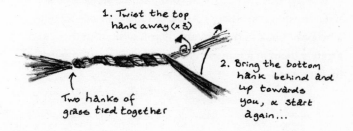

1. Twist the top hank away (x 3)

Two hanks of grass tied together

2. Bring the bottom hank behind and up towards you, & start again...

Pressing Matters

While browsing in a second-hand bookshop one day, I came across a copy of *The Language of Flowers or Flora Symbolica* from 1887. I bought it and took it home, where I discovered scores of dried flowers and leaves pressed within its pages like antique bookmarks. Wonderful to think they might have survived for more than 130 years.

To dry your own flowers, ferns and leaves, pick them fresh in the morning once the dew has evaporated. (Please don't pull up any wild flowers by the roots, or pick any endangered plants.) Flowers with flat faces such as violets work well, as do buttercups, daisies and wild grasses.

Place the freshly picked flowers between two sheets of white paper and put this inside a heavy book, such as a dictionary. Moisture from the flowers might make the pages wrinkle, so use a book you don't mind damaging and, if drying multiple flowers, space them out inside. Close the book and put a weight or a pile of other books on top to keep the pages flat. Then leave this in a dry, cool place for a couple of weeks.

The dried flowers will be fragile, so handle them delicately. You could glue them here in your journal, along with a note of when and where you picked them, or use them in a bespoke bookmark or a card. If you wish, trim them and arrange them in a transparent glass frame as a reminder of bright days.

Picked on _____

at _____

EARTH

Walk the Land

The Aboriginal people of Australia navigate their land through age-old songlines or dreaming tracks, mythological paths whose sacred landmarks are recorded in song. This means that if you know the rhythm of the song, you know the land. While not the same thing, Alfred Watkins came up with the term 'ley line' in 1921 to describe the straight tracks that supposedly link ancient sites in Britain. These ley lines, in turn, came to be associated with mystical energy pathways.

Pilgrims, of course, walk to their holy destinations. Is there perhaps a quality about walking itself that invokes a sense of the sacred, with the rhythm of the feet, the thumping of the heart, the looseness of the limbs?

Create a connected walk of your own. Choose two spots some distance apart that appeal or seem significant to you in some way. Walk between them in as straight a line as you can, while keeping to permitted rights of way. Make a mental note on your journey of what you see and any landmarks along the way. Listen to your footsteps. Perhaps you will be inspired to craft a song of your own?

The Wonder of Weeds

While there are weeds such as hemlock and poison ivy that you wouldn't welcome into your living space, others can bring benefits. Some weeds help check soil erosion and add organic matter and nutrients to the soil, while others with long roots can help break up compacted ground – the weed equivalent of earthworms.

The shrub buddleia can seed itself, weed-like, in wasteland, and is known as the butterfly bush for good reason. In summer, buddleia can become a fluttering heaven of butterfly wings as the insects flit about, sipping on the flowers. Even ivy, often ripped off walls and trees, is an important food supply for honeybees and birds in the autumn because of its late flowering season and calorie-rich berries.

If washed and prepared, weeds can be nutritious for human beings too. Add hot (not boiling) water to cleavers, also known as goose grass, for a medicinal cup of herbal tea that's good for the digestive system. Or make yourself a salad from young dandelion leaves or chickweed, with its tiny white flowers. For a hot dish, sauté nettles, chickweed or sorrel with a little garlic and olive oil, and serve with a drizzle of lemon.

—— ∞ ——

'A weed is but an unloved flower.'
ELLA WHEELER WILCOX (1850–1919), 'The Weed'

Colour Quest

While it might not always seem like it on an overcast day, nature is bursting with colour. Even if you look closely at a cloud, you will notice different hues – pale pinks and lilacs, or steely blues. We are surrounded by colour even in the most built-up of spaces, from the pearlescent shimmer of a pigeon's neck to the startling yellow sunbursts of dandelions growing in the pavement cracks. How many different shades of green, for instance, do you notice once you really start to look?

To open your artist's eye, choose a colour for the day and make a mental note each time you spot it. Colours serve many functions in the natural world, such as camouflage and protection, as well as enticement for pollination or attracting mates, and they also tend to evoke particular cultural meanings.

If you feel inspired by what you see, sketch something here in your journal that captures colour; it could be orange lichen on a rock, the pink inside a shell or rough brown crumbling wood – whatever catches your eye.

What does colour mean to you?

———— ∞ ————

'Every particular in nature, a leaf, a drop, a crystal, a moment of time is related to the whole, and partakes of the perfection of the whole.'

RALPH WALDO EMERSON (1803–1882),
Nature, Addresses and Lectures

Capturing colour

EARTH

Sky

ather poetically, the sky is known in astronomy as the celestial sphere or celestial dome. In a way, it protects life on Earth rather like a gardener's glass cloche shields plants, creating the perfect conditions for them to grow. As well as sheltering us, the sky is a constant reminder of the great potential that surrounds us – the immense universe with its billions of heavenly bodies, from meteorites to planets. Our Sun is but one star among many.

The sky invites us to look up and face the horizon – from witnessing dawn and dusk, to reading the phases of the Moon. While we cannot control the weather, we can learn to meet it with equanimity and benefit from whatever it might bring, sunshine or showers. For who knows what wonders will arrive upon the wind?

'Clouds come floating into my life, no longer to carry rain or usher storm, but to add colour to my sunset sky.'

RABINDRANATH TAGORE (1861–1941), *Stray Birds*

From Dawn till Dusk

For a week or two during the year, make a point of witnessing the sunrise and sunset. During the summer, you may have to keep longer hours to do this, whereas winter days are shorter. Any time of the year, though, offers its rewards – from June mornings veiled in mist to the fiery skies of a December dusk.

Make a note of where the Sun rises and sets in the sky, as this will give you your east and west.

The old weather saying goes: 'Red sky in the morning, shepherd's warning; red sky at night, shepherd's delight.' (Or 'gasworks are on fire', according to my grandad.) There is some truth to this, as most weather systems arrive from the west, and a red sky at night is often a sign that high pressure is on its way, bringing fair weather with it. However, a red sky in the morning means the weather system has already passed through, and rain and wind might follow on its tails.

As well as discovering how dawn and dusk act as bookends to shore up a day, see whether they offer you any clues about what's to come in the hours ahead.

Sun Printing

Sun or solar printing owes its origins to two extraordinary individuals. In 1841, the English astronomer and scientist Sir John Herschel invented the cyanotype printing process, which he used mainly to reproduce notes and plans – the prototype of architectural 'blueprints'. Two years later, botanist Anna Atkins became the first person to publish a book of photographic images, which she did using cyanotypes of ferns and algae. She created the images by placing her specimens directly onto a specially prepared sheet of paper and allowing the action of direct sunlight to create silhouettes.

Sun printing is very easy to do, and the results can be stunning. To make your own prints, you will need:

* A sheet of sun-print paper (available online and from craft stores).
* A range of objects with interesting outlines, such as ferns, feathers and small flowers.
* A piece of cardboard and a sheet of plexiglass or glass; or an old clip frame will do.
* Clips for holding cardboard, paper and glass together.
* A sunny day – a bright winter's day will work fine.
* A container of cold water for washing your print.

Indoors, out of direct sunlight, place a sheet of sun-print paper blue side up on the cardboard.

Carefully arrange your objects on the paper.

Flatten the objects into place with the plexiglass or glass, and attach the clips to hold everything together. (The clips will appear in the final image, so keep them at the edge where they can be trimmed off.)

Go outside and hold the objects up to the bright sunlight, or prop the whole caboodle where the sunlight will fall on it without casting shadows over the paper. Leave it in the sunlight for about five minutes, or until the paper has changed colour.

Once the paper around the objects has changed colour to white or a very light blue, bring your image indoors.

Remove and rinse the sheet of sun-print paper in cold water for about a minute. The colours on the print will begin to reverse.

Leave the paper to dry. As it dries the print will darken.

Display your finished print, or glue it in your journal.

If, at first, you don't succeed, have another go!

S K Y

Blue Sky Mind

The next sunny day that comes along, give yourself
permission to relax outdoors for a few moments. Turn
off any distracting gadgets and make yourself comfortable.
You might like to sit with both feet on the ground and your
hands resting in your lap, or lie flat on your back, gazing up
at the sky.

Face in a direction where you won't be dazzled by
sunshine, yet can watch the clouds overhead. And breathe.

There's no need to breathe in any particular way or to try
to control your breath. Just inhale and exhale softly.

Keeping your awareness on your breath, let any thoughts
drift away from you like the clouds passing overhead, on
their way elsewhere. If thoughts and worries keep coming
back to pester you like so many cawing crows, turn your
attention once more to the clouds. Look for any shapes
and the way the light falls on them.

After a few minutes of mindfulness, slowly return to
daily life.

Cloud Factory

On an overcast day there are likely to be many different types of cloud jostling for position in the sky. There are ten main genera, all with different names depending on their appearance and altitude, the three basic ones being:

* *Stratus* (after the Latin *strato*, for layer): these are low blankets of featureless cloud that often bring drizzle or light snow; nimbostratus is a thick swathe of rain-bearing cloud – dark and gloomy.

* *Cumulus* (after the Latin *cumulo*, for heap or pile): flat-bottomed and fluffy, these are the heaps of cotton wool that appear on sunny days, and can be a sign of rain to come. The saying goes, 'In the morning, mountains; in the evening, fountains.'

* *Cirrus* (after the Latin *cirrus*, for a curl of hair): made of ice crystals, and often a sign of changeable weather, these clouds are high up and wispy, and can form white mares' tails.

Keep an eye on the sky and see if you can predict the weather from the clouds approaching in the distance. The World Meterological Organisation recently named 12 new cloud types, making these the first additions to the International Cloud Atlas for 30 years. Even cloud spotting offers fresh discoveries.

Pine Cones and Seaweed

By the time he died in 2004 at the age of 91, Bill Foggitt was Britain's best-known amateur weather forecaster, with a wide range of interesting techniques at his disposal – from using drowsy flies to predict thunderstorms, to being able to tell if rain was on the way when flowers such as scarlet pimpernel began to close. Most of his methods seem to boil down to a close observation of the natural world.

If you'd like to predict the weather yourself, you can of course poke your head outside and take a look. Or you could keep a pine cone on a ledge outdoors. In fair weather, the outside of the cone's scales will become drier than the interior and the cone will open – allowing the wind to catch any seeds and disperse them in favourable conditions. Whereas if rain is on the way, the outside of the cone's scales will absorb moisture and swell shut. Even when all the seeds have dispersed, the cone will carry on opening and closing according to humidity levels.

If you're nautically inclined, hang a piece of seaweed by your front door. It'll become damp if rain is on the way. However, it might also dampen if dew is forming, so it isn't quite as reliable as a landlubber's trusty cone.

Let It Rain

One wet winter's day, I was hurrying along with all the other shoppers, heads down, hunched, when a flash of iridescent blue caught my eye as I was crossing a bridge. A kingfisher was below, darting from perch to perch to fish the river in the rain. Not a sight I'd expected to see in the city centre. I stood, watching and marvelling, and the moment felt like a gift.

When I was much younger, a sudden downpour filled the streets and washed away my shoes. I gave up trying to keep them on my feet and sploshed along barefoot with my friend Kath, both of us laughing like drains as we were applauded by crowds sheltering in shopfronts.

Rain can of course cause devastation in the form of floods, but it's also a life-giving force. And it will come when it will come. My father once knew a manufacturer in Ireland who sold bottled water, and who would rush outside laughing, 'Supplies are coming in!' when the heavens opened.

None of us can change the weather, but we can be open to the good that it might bring.

———— ∞ ————

'For after all, the best thing one can do
When it is raining is to let it rain.'

HENRY WADSWORTH LONGFELLOW (1807–1882),
'The Poet's Tale'

Rainbow's End

Whenever I see a rainbow, I find myself trying to imagine where it ends, as though I might one day discover a leprechaun's pot of gold at its foot. Created by the refraction of light, rainbows appear in the sky opposite the Sun, with the top of the arc at about a 42° angle to your own shadow. In a single rainbow, red appears on the outside of the arc and violet on its inside; to remember the order of the colours, there's the handy mnemonic: Richard Of York Gave Battle In Vain (red, orange, yellow, green, blue, indigo, violet). However, if you're lucky enough to see a double rainbow, the order will be reversed in the outer, secondary arc.

If you'd like to add a little more colour to your life, create your own rainbows by placing a glass of water above a piece of white paper in strong sunlight; or, in a dark room, lean a mirror at an angle in a glass of water and shine a torch on the part of the mirror that's under water.

To play with light in other ways, make a Sun catcher. Pour a 5 mm (¼ in) layer of clear-drying PVA glue into a flexible round plastic lid or shallow plastic container. Onto this, arrange a flat layer of florist's glass pebbles until there's room for no more, then dribble a little more glue on top and allow to dry for three or four days. When it's set, peel the Sun catcher out of the lid and, using ribbon or fishing line, hang it up to the light.

Fog Blanket

Formed from water droplets or ice crystals, fog can seem like a lingering cloud too lazy to take to the sky and drift away. While it may lead to hazardous driving conditions, it transforms a landscape, wrapping it in swathes of white, muffling and distorting sounds, and, in the right conditions, creating spooky three-dimensional shadows.

If you venture out in fog, the world can feel very strange. I once came across a digger in the woods, which, hidden in mist, resembled a creature woken from legend, roaring and lumbering. Fog clings to your skin, clothing and hair, beading them in moisture; it makes it hard to judge distances or to tell what's really there. Yet it can appear and disperse in a moment, like a magician's cloth.

When fog next arrives, step into it and be aware of how it fills your senses. In what ways does it change your relationship with your surroundings? Make a note in your journal to describe the experience.

A Halo of Ice

The saying goes that a 'ring around the Moon means rain or snow soon', and there's a measure of truth in this. A lunar halo or Moon ring is created by the reflection and refraction of moonlight in ice crystals in the upper atmosphere. At high altitude, ice crystals can form cirrus or cirrostratus clouds, which can be a sign that stormy weather is approaching.

As the ring around the Moon is set at an angle of approximately 22° relative to the observer, this phenomenon is also known as a 22° halo. If you're lucky enough to witness it, see if you can capture it on camera or sketch it. And look for colours – you might find blue and red in the night's answer to a rainbow.

Waxing or Waning?

Here's a very simple trick to work out whether the Moon is waxing or waning.

First, wait for the Moon to rise in the night sky.

If you live in the Northern Hemisphere, hold your right hand up to the sky, over the Moon, and curve your fingers into a reversed C-shape. If the illuminated side of the Moon fits into the curve of your right hand, the Moon is waxing and will increase in size until it's gloriously full.

However, if the illuminated side of the Moon fits into your left (or 'sinister') hand, it's waning and has already been full.

While the phases of the Moon are the same all around the Earth, if you live in the Southern Hemisphere, the Moon will fit into the C-shape of your left hand when waxing, and into your right when waning.

—— ∞ ——

'A savage place! as holy and enchanted
As e'er beneath a waning moon was haunted ...'

SAMUEL TAYLOR COLERIDGE (1772–1834),
Kubla Khan

Earthshine

When there's a waxing crescent Moon, the rest of the Moon can sometimes be faintly seen bathed in a soft light. This effect is called 'earthshine', caused by sunlight reflecting off the Earth and onto the Moon. It's also known as the Moon's 'ashen glow', or 'the old Moon in the new Moon's arms', as the best time to see it is on the first few nights just before or after a new Moon. The phenomenon was first described by Leonardo da Vinci in the early 1500s and, among others, inspired landscape painter Samuel Palmer (1805–1881) in his study *The Harvest Moon*.

Earthshine glows more dimly than the Moon's crescent, as the light has been reflected twice. It is also affected by the Moon's albedo – how much sunlight the Moon can reflect. The Moon's albedo is lower than the Earth's: where the Earth reflects back 30 per cent of the sunlight that hits its surface, the Moon only reflects back 12 per cent. This means the Earth would look many times brighter to someone on the Moon than a full Moon does to an earthling.

At night, keep an eye out for earthshine. During the day, focus for a while on reflections, and the way light bounces back from surfaces or colours shadows. What effects do you see?

Moon Walk

My mother was a midwife and would anticipate a full Moon with a certain amount of trepidation, as the labour ward was reputedly especially busy at this time of the month. Not only were more births thought to occur at a full Moon, but wounds were believed to bleed more profusely, and some people were convinced there were more incidents of violence and insanity – or lunacy (which comes from the Latin *lunaticus*, from *luna* – 'moon'). The jury is out about whether any of this has any basis in fact, but I guess it does go to show how jittery we instinctively feel about a full Moon.

And yet, and yet . . . how beautiful the night appears when the sky is cloudless and the Moon full, and everything is cast in silver. Some moonlit nights can be bright enough for a night walk, so perhaps the next splendid full Moon will inspire you to go out for a late evening stroll, when you might well encounter nocturnal animals such as bats and badgers. Walking through fields at night, I once heard a chorus of nightjars burst spontaneously into song as the Moon emerged from behind the clouds.

If you do decide to go for a moonlit walk, please exercise a degree of caution, keep your wits about you and don't take any unnecessary risks. That said, I have known people strip off to their underwear and run round fields, hugging trees, under the influence of a beautiful Moon. However, like any activity in this book, tree-hugging in your pants is, of course, entirely optional.

Dream Diary

I've recently started to keep a dream diary that includes the phases of the Moon. Don't worry, I'm not about to bore you with the details . . . although they are fascinating . . .

While few of us find other people's dreams interesting, most of us are intrigued by our own, and it would be nice to know if they tally with lunar phases in any way – especially as there's such a strong link between the Moon and human behaviour in mythology and folklore. As human beings are composed of about 60 per cent water, it's natural to wonder if the Moon might affect us in the same way it does tides, although there are no scientific findings to date (that I'm aware of) to suggest it does. I know I'm often restless on nights with a full Moon, but that could simply be because of the light filtering in through the curtains – I'm not sure.

It's still early days in terms of relating my dreams to lunar phases, but I've been enjoying finding out what's been going on in my subconscious: working through problems, shifting through emotions, having wild adventures. You can easily discover the benefits yourself by buying a Moon diary or creating your own. All you will need are a blank journal, a table of lunar phases (available online), a pen by your bedside – and a willingness to write down your dreams on waking. You could make a start here, in your journal. After three or four months have elapsed, read through to see if there's any connection between your dreams and the rest of your life, as well as the Moon. Do you discover any patterns?

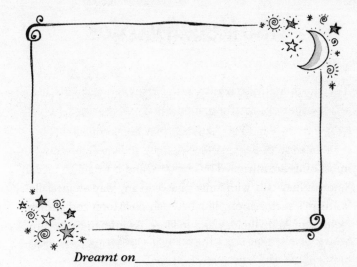

*Dreamt on*_____

when the Moon was _____

*Dreamt on*_____

when the Moon was _____

S K Y

The Steadfast Star

The North Star, also known as the Pole Star or Polaris, has a long history as an important navigational marker. This lodestar, used by sailors to guide the course of their ships, marks true north and seems to remain stationary in the northern sky as other stars rotate round it. The further north you travel, the higher the North Star appears to climb above the horizon, until it sits directly overhead at the North Pole. However, the further south you head, the lower the North Star appears in the sky, completely disappearing from view in the Southern Hemisphere.

To find the North Star, search the northern night sky for a constellation that looks like a dipped saucepan: Ursa Major (also known as the Great Bear, Plough or Big Dipper). Take the distance between the two stars at the blunt end of Ursa Major and multiply this by five, tracing upwards from the tip of the constellation in a straight line, and using the two stars as pointers towards the North Star. The North Star is the brightest star in the constellation of Ursa Minor (the Little Bear or Little Dipper) and forms the end of that pan-like constellation's handle.

If you were attempting to find your way at night, how might this star help you?

———— ∞ ————

'Bright star, would I were stedfast as thou art'

JOHN KEATS (1795–1821), 'Bright Star'

Shooting Stars

I was once invited to a dinner with a difference. Our host had set the table outside so we could enjoy a special light show: a meteor shower trailing through the night sky.

Meteor showers are formed by tiny particles of debris left in the wake of passing comets, and are named after the constellation in which they appear to originate (known as their radiant) – a clue where to find them in the sky. In the Northern Hemisphere, one of the best times to catch them is in late July through to mid-August, when the Perseids reach their peak. December is also a good month, as this is when the Geminids, Ursids and Quadrantids blaze through the sky. Those in the Southern Hemisphere can catch the Eta Aquarids caused by Halley's Comet in late April to mid-May.

To enjoy a meteor shower, wrap up warm and find a dark spot. Even the brightness of the Moon can affect visibility, so a clear night with a new Moon is best. Make yourself comfortable in a reclining chair or be prepared to crick your neck as you scour the heavens. Then settle down and wait. It might take a while to get your eye in, but if you're lucky you'll be rewarded. At their height, the Perseids can produce over fifty meteors an hour – and that's a lot of shooting stars to wish on.

Turn to Face the Wind

Winds are named for the direction from which they have come, rather than where they're heading. The north wind, for instance, originates in the north and blows towards the south. Generally speaking, in the Northern Hemisphere:

* The north wind and east winds are cold (think of blasts of air heading across from Siberia).
* The south and particularly west winds are seen as mild and favourable, coming from more temperate oceanic climes.

However, winds take on the properties of the areas they have crossed. The north wind is hot in the Southern Hemisphere, for example, and can cause bush fires in Australia.

To gauge the direction of the wind, turn towards it until it feels as though it's blowing straight at you, hitting you full in the face with an equal amount of blast in each ear. Then look for a landmark to help you get your bearings. Or, if you have access to a compass – perhaps on your phone – check that. Seagulls tend to stand facing into the wind, whereas cows prefer to stand with their backsides towards it, sensible things.

As you become familiar with the wind directions, make a note of any difference in their properties, such as the weather fronts they bring with them or any different smells in the air, and jot down your findings.

Go Fly a Kite

Kites were invented in ancient China, and made from silk or paper and bamboo. Far from being toys, they were originally used by the military to measure distances and wind speeds, and for signalling. Nevertheless, an airborne kite appears a playful thing when it's dancing in the breeze.

To make a simple kite, you will need:

* A pen and an A4 sheet of paper
* Scissors
* A piece of wrapping paper approximately 33 by 33 cm (13 × 13 in)
* Two thin sticks (e.g. bamboo kebab skewers), approximately 25 cm (10 in) long
* Masking tape or sticky tape
* Thin string or fishing line

To make your template, measure down 10.5 cm (4⅕ in) from the top of the A4 paper (in portrait) and draw a horizontal line of 15 cm (6 in). Measure 10 cm (4 in) along this and bisect it with a vertical line of 29 cm (11½ in). Join

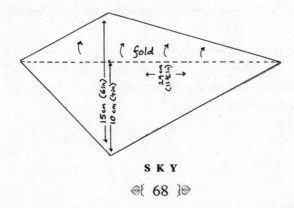

S K Y

up the ends of the cross with four straight lines to create a lopsided kite shape and cut this out.

Fold the wrapping paper in half. Place the bottom-right edge of the template against the fold and cut round it so that when you open the paper, it looks like a heart with straight edges. Fold the left side of the paper heart halfway over the right side and tape it into place to create a diamond kite shape.

Tape one stick into place vertically down the centre of the kite. Tape the other horizontally across and trim the ends.

Using the leftover paper, make three or four strips approximately 20 cm long by 1 cm wide (8 × ½ in) and tape these to the base for a tail.

Turn the kite over. Add another bit of tape, if you like, to strengthen the flap at the centre of the kite, before piercing it and attaching the string.

Go outside on a breezy day and stand with your back to the wind. Release your kite up into the air and let it fly away from you a little before pulling on the string to make it climb (hopefully) higher and higher . . .

Good luck!

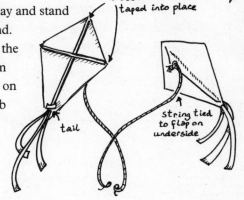

crossed sticks taped into place

tail

string tied to flap on underside

Storm Watching

The skies darken with billowing clouds and the wind picks up from a whisper, whipping water into waves and howling through the trees. Storms can be exhilarating and dazzling spectacles to watch, as though the elements have decided to unleash their power and prove what they can do.

Storm watching has become big business in some parts of the world, with organised adventure tours chasing tornadoes and supercell thunderstorms in areas of the States. Besides incredible landscapes, these offer the thrill of the hunt and a sense of camaraderie on the road.

To go storm watching, wrap up warm and find a safe vantage point from which you can't, for instance, be swept out to sea by a freak wave. If there's any threat of lightning, stay indoors (keeping away from electrical appliances and plumbing pipes) or remain in a car to watch the action.

Enjoy the ever-evolving skyscapes and their combination of beauty, threat and mystery – the distant colours of the horizon, the changing light and towering clouds, and bands of approaching rain or hail. Take photos or video recordings, or simply describe the experience as best you can.

—— ∞ ——

'There are some things you learn best in calm,
and some in storm.'

WILLA CATHER (1873–1947), *The Song of the Lark*

Spider Flight

A friend once told me she'd seen lines of energy shimmering across a field. Perhaps she had, although I wonder if the glittering threads she'd spotted were actually fine threads of spiders' webs catching the morning light.

The silk woven by spiders is an incredible substance. Stronger, weight for weight, than steel, it has multiple uses in a spider's life – from reproduction and raising spiderlings, to catching prey and storing it, to travelling across oceans. Even tiny money spiders can perform ballooning, or kiting, when they release a thread of silk so that the breeze can pick them up and carry them off to a new home. If fields become covered with this sort of gossamer web from migrating spiders, the phenomenon is known as 'angel hair'.

Should you find an unoccupied web (having made sure its owner isn't hiding nearby), you can preserve it for posterity. First, colour the web with spray paint if you wish, holding a sheet of paper behind it to make sure you don't spray anything else, or alternatively powder the web with talc or cornflour. Then quickly coat a piece of card with hairspray or spray mount to make it tacky, and sweep this up behind the web, lifting so the web breaks free from its moorings. Once you've successfully transferred the web to the card, you can preserve it with another layer of hair spray or a thin coat of clear varnish.

Or you could just draw the web in situ, leaving it to catch the next day's dew.

Water

Seen from space, the Earth looks like a swirling blue marble, for 71 per cent of the planet's surface is covered by water. Similarly, water is the major component of our bodies, and we share our fundamental dependency on it with all other living organisms – from bacteria to blue whales.

Water sustains us in so many different ways. In his poem 'Water', Philip Larkin describes how, if he were to 'construct a religion', he would build it around the element of water. The next time you drink a glass, enjoy a moment of calm by slowly paying attention to each sip you take. To experience water in its element, explore the waterways that snake through the land around you and discover the life within them. Go wild swimming and relax to the sound of the lapping waves.

Let water wash away your worries and restore you to yourself.

— ∞ —

'Nothing is softer or more yielding than water,
yet to attack the hard and strong, nothing can surpass it.'

Lao Tzu (c.604–531 bc), *Tao Te Ching*

WATER

Go Fishing – Without a Rod

My grandad was a very keen fisherman, as was his father, Charlie. The story goes that Grandad was on his way to an angling competition when a friendly acquaintance stopped to ask him how Charlie was, having not seen him at any matches for a while. 'Oh, he had a bit of bad luck yesterday,' said Grandad. 'He died.'

Now, you could put this phlegmatic attitude down to the fact that Grandad was (a) a Yorkshireman, and (b) nothing was going to get in the way of his fishing. For an immensely talkative soul, Grandad spent an awful lot of time sitting in silence on the riverbank, thinking his thoughts and watching the world flow by. He knew where to find kingfishers, dragonflies and water voles, as well as fish, and the best spots for casting. When we were small, my brothers and I would sit alongside him with rods made of sticks tied with string, and it was wonderful to see the river through his eyes.

It seems to me, having spoken to various anglers over the years, that a hot mug of tea is an essential piece of fishing kit, and some use a Kelly Kettle to brew up on the riverbank. To keep things simple, I'd suggest simply packing a Thermos flask full of a hot drink or soup in cold weather, or something refreshing on a warm day. Then take yourself down to the bankside – whether river, stream, canal or ornamental pond. Quietly stake your place and take your time. Who knows what your catch will be?

Skimming Stones

Skimming (or skipping) stones is a skill it's never too late to acquire. The best places to skim are smooth expanses of water, such as a calm sea, a still loch or lake, reservoir, stretch of river or broad canal without boats or swimmers in the way. Even a large pond will do if you can find some decent-sized pebbles and don't scare the ducks.

First, you'll need to find the right type of stone, so take a good look round. Ideally, the stone should be thin and flat like a small piece of slate, and not too heavy or lumpy or it will sink straightaway.

If you're right-handed, make a backwards C-shape or U-shape with your index finger and thumb. Your stone should fit snugly into the crook of that space, but don't grip it too hard.

When you go to throw it, pull back your hand and flick the stone sharply forwards with your wrist as you release it. Instead of lobbing the stone upwards so it sinks with a splash, the idea is to set it spinning like a flat disc in a straight line towards the water. It might help to crouch down so you're at the right level. Then, with luck, your stone will skim across the surface a number of times before sinking.

Stone skimming is a companionable thing to do – and it can be highly competitive, with international stone-skimming championships. The world record, set in 2013, is 88 skims; although the most I've ever achieved is ten, I think. These days I'm a bit out of practice, yet I still try to skim a stone or two whenever I visit the beach in winter.

Dowsing

Dowsing is the ancient art of searching for water or minerals hidden underground, which can be practised by anyone, anywhere.

The grandmother of a friend of mine lived just off the inner ringroad in a genteel cathedral city. Mrs H was quite a down-to-earth lady – much more likely to attend her local bridge club than a pagan moot, for example. Yet, when a hapless team from the local water authority struggled to fix a problem with her drains, Mrs H came to the rescue.

Try as they might, using charts and gadgets, the team were unable to locate the faulty drain. With a sigh, Mrs H looked round her garden for a forked branch. She then held the branch loosely in front of her, at arm's length, and focused. Following the 'pull' of the branch, within a minute she had correctly dowsed the location of the pipe underground in her gravel driveway.

Hazel, willow and peach are said to make particularly good dowsing rods. But you can also use two pieces of L-shaped wire fashioned from an old coat hanger. Hold the wire rods loosely in each hand so they point straight ahead, take a couple of deep breaths to relax and walk forward slowly. Be aware of any unusual sensations in your hands, such as the rods feeling 'jumpy'.

If the wire rods unexpectedly swing in to cross over each other, X marks the spot and you may well have found a water source underfoot.

Take a Dip

Wild swimming involves taking a dip in natural waters such as lakes and rivers. There is something delicious about swimming in the open air on a hot summer's day, with the sky reflected on the surface and your arms and legs drifting lazily like water weeds. Animals usually give wild swimmers a wide berth, although ducks will often paddle among the reeds close by, unflappable, while dragonflies and other insects dart overhead.

I once swam in a pond in Italy that was fed by thermal springs, and every now and then I would float into a warm spot, to be surprised by bubbles. I think the local anglers were probably even more surprised to find a *donna inglese* bobbing about in their usual spot, and I clambered out as soon as they set up their kit. Swimming and fishing aren't a good mix.

I am, I admit, very much a fair-weather wild swimmer. Seasoned wild swimmers will pull on their wetsuits and head out come rain or shine, sometimes travelling for miles to visit a new waterway, as the experience can become addictive. If wild swimming appeals to you, there are some practical guidelines about safety, access and behaving responsibly that you'll find listed on most good wild swimming websites.

So why not tense your toes and take a dip on the wild side? You could emerge refreshed in more ways than one.

As Nature Intended

The first time I went swimming naked was by mistake. We were walking towards a beach in the north of Spain when my husband commented, 'Funny, isn't it, how everyone's wearing beige swimming trunks?' They weren't. Fifteen hot, flustered and fully-clothed minutes later, it became apparent we'd be much less conspicuous if we just got on with it and stripped off too. Swimming in the warm sea was like relaxing in a bath under a blue sky – just wonderful.

Taking off your clothes in public isn't everybody's cup of tea – certainly not in Britain. However, people tend to be much more laid-back about such matters on the continent. In the parks and lakes of Berlin, for example, it's quite usual to see people unwinding after work in the all-together.

If you'd like to shed your inhibitions along with the layers, there are many recognised naturist spots around the world, including in the heart of cities and at swimming clubs. Do a little research to find out what's nearby. Then, making sure you respect the attitudes of other people and follow the local etiquette, experience what it's like to return to nature in the raw.

Row a Boat

In the children's classic *The Wind in the Willows*, Mole and Rat set out one night in a rowing boat to search for a missing child. On the very brink of dawn, they are rewarded with a vision of the pagan god Pan piping 'heavenly music'. It's a curious episode, conjuring up the pure sense of wonder and connection that can come from spending time in nature – especially when gliding along a river.

Rowing, however, is quite hard work. To row a boat, put on a lifejacket and step down into the middle of the rowing boat carefully, keeping your weight low. Sit with your back to the bow (front) and make sure the boat doesn't list to either side.

With the oars secured in the rowlocks, dip both blades in the water, but not too deep. Pull back with your arms, circling upwards as your hands come towards you, then downwards as you push away to propel the blades through the water. To turn, row using only the oar on the side of the direction you want to go in (e.g. right oar to turn right). To stop, dig both blades into the water, straightening your arms.

While there are no guarantees you'll bump into any deities on the riverbank, a rowing boat will allow you to explore the secret inlets and tiny islands that nobody else can reach.

———— ∞ ————

'There is nothing – absolutely nothing – half so much worth doing as simply messing about in boats.'

KENNETH GRAHAME (1859–1932), *The Wind in the Willows*

A Tribute to Tributaries

Some years ago, I fell into conversation with an elderly gentleman striding through a field on the outskirts of the village. He introduced himself as Mr Painter, the Dorset River Tramp, gave me his card and explained he was on a quest to trace the vast network of tributaries that feeds the county of Dorset's rivers. He now had the farmer's permission to cross his land to investigate a particular stream.

Later, I looked at the map and discovered there was indeed a spring nearby, and the stream flowed past our cottage to merge a few miles later with the picturesque River Stour. One of our neighbours had recently rigged up a tripwire camera to catch the culprit stealing his Koi carp (the neighbour was a retired Met police officer and a dab hand at surveillance), and had caught a dog otter in the act. This now made sense, as the otter could easily have swum upstream from the river.

Wherever your home – city or shire – the chances are you live near a waterway of some kind. Look on a map and trace this watercourse's path to find out where it leads and where it originates. Is it fed by, or does it feed into, any streams, brooks, rivers or lakes? If you can, visit a couple of these locations to get a sense of the hidden river network that surrounds you. Before you set out, jot down your thoughts about what you expect to find, then compare these to the reality you discover.

Wending Rivers

Streams and rivers form natural wildlife corridors, enabling animals to move from one habitat to another. The life in a stretch of waterway is influenced by the land it makes its way through; upland waters, for instance, tend to be nutrient poor compared with those downstream, and are likely to be more affected by rainfall and snowmelt. However, every plant or animal in a watery habitat has to cope with flowing water.

Depending on the depth and strength of the current (and wildlife – don't try this if there are any crocodiles about), one way to get to know a stream or shallow river is to pull on your boots and wade out into it. Err on the side of caution: if the current feels strong or it's slippery underfoot, turn back. If the going is easy, follow the course of the water upstream and, depending on the time of year and location, look for beetles, spiders, water boatmen, damselflies and dragonflies. Keep an eye out for the flitting shapes of fish and waterfowl. And what of the ground under your feet – is it rocky, shingle or sand? Search for tell-tale signs of small mammals such as voles in the banks. Look for wildflowers.

And be prepared for surprises. I once came across a huge dead eel wedged in a narrow stream. Strange to think it had ended its days there, thousands of miles from its birthplace in the Sargasso Sea.

Snake in the Grass

The largest British reptile is the grass snake, also known as the ringed snake or water snake. A non-venomous, brownish-grey-green snake with a yellow collar, it feeds on amphibians and can be found along waterways, as well as in hedgerows and meadows.

From a boat, I once watched two magnificent grass snakes swim out from an island – they must have been several feet long. Another time, a tiny juvenile grass snake wriggled its way into our home. I have no idea how it got there, but the dog was terrified. Fascinated, yet nevertheless a bit disconcerted, I scooped the snake into a beer glass and released it outside.

A fear of snakes and spiders seems to be instinctive – and with good reason, as there are many species around the world whose bite can prove lethal. However, it's worth examining the kneejerk reaction we often have to those aspects of nature that unsettle us.

If you can bear it, have a think about what you find frightening, disturbing or repulsive about the natural world. How logical is that response and how might it influence your general attitude to nature?

The Toad's Hidden Jewel

All toads are frogs, but not all frogs are toads – and that's the truth of it. Toads are a type of frog; both are members of the order Anura, but true toads belong to a separate family within it (however, the word 'toad' has no meaning within scientific taxonomy; poor toads – ignored by science, yet recognised by the people). Where frogs lay eggs in clusters, toads lay theirs in chains. Toads crawl and frogs hop. Frogs tend to have long webbed hind feet and damp skin compared to the squatter, drier, bumpy-skinned toad with its poisonous paratoid glands.

It seems easier to love a lithe frog than a dumpy toad; you can see why fairy-tale princesses prefer them. Yet good looks aren't everything. According to myth, the toad possesses a secret treasure – a gem in its head, or toadstone – which is supposedly an antidote to poison. In her poem 'Lullaby for a Baby Toad', Stella Gibbons describes a mother toad assuring her child that the reason for its ugliness is to protect the hidden 'jewel that shines / In the flat toad-head' from jealous mankind.

Quickly jot down a list of any creatures or plants you find it particularly difficult to like, let alone love. (I'm guessing wasps might feature on quite a few people's lists.) Then do a little research. Do they have any redeeming qualities?

A couple of summers ago, we had a hornets' nest above our backdoor, but once we'd learned a bit about them and how to live with them, everybody got along just fine . . .

Pond Life

An outdoor water feature will encourage nature to come to you. But you don't have to dig a lake. Just create a pond in a pot. All you'll need are:

* A clean, watertight container with a nonreactive surface – a tin tub, plastic bucket or large frost-proof bowl will do. If using half a wooden barrel, line it with plastic liner to prevent rot and potentially harmful chemicals leaching into the water.
* Bricks (depending on the depth of your container) and pebbles.
* Water. Collected rainwater is best, although tap water is fine.
* A variety of plants, including floaters such as frogbit, oxygenators such as water crowfoot and marginals such as yellow flag. (Some aquatic plants aren't frost hardy, so will need to be replaced in spring after the last frost unless you bring the pot pond indoors to overwinter.) For a container with a diameter of approximately 40 cm (16 in) and depth of 30 cm (12 in), you'll need about four or five plants.

Put the container in a partially sunny spot and, if needed, place the bricks inside around the edge to raise the plants to the right level. Partially fill the container with water.

If your plants are already in planting baskets, simply position these around the edges. If they're in pots, replant them in planting baskets using aquatic compost and cover the compost with a fine layer of pea gravel. Don't overfill the pond with plants: allow them space to grow.

Make a ramp from pebbles or add a feature stone to ensure wildlife can get in and out easily, then top up the water to about 2–3 cm (1 in) below the rim. Fish will eat other pond life, but if you'd like to add a couple, wait a fortnight to let the water stabilise.

When there's a couple of inches of decomposed matter at the bottom of the pond, drain it and scrub it clean, dividing up plants if necessary.

Enjoy the wildlife that your homemade oasis will attract.

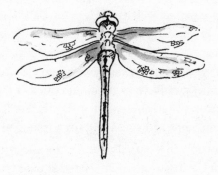

Going Underground

Sometimes even mighty rivers go underground. They might be naturally subterranean, as with the network of rivers discovered in 2014 under Galway Bay, Ireland; or they could have been buried by urban development. London's polluted Fleet and Effra were completely built over by the mid to late nineteenth century, and incorporated into the city's drainage and sewage system. At roughly the same time, New York's Sunswick Creek and Minetta Brook suffered a similar fate, as did Tank Stream in Sydney.

The trend is being reversed today by daylighting or de-culverting, whereby a waterway is restored to a more natural state. Saw Mill River in Yonkers, New York, has been freed from a parking lot (a bit like the remains of Richard III), and one of the great rivers in the north of England, the River Medlock, is currently being reclaimed from the culverts.

Clues to the presence of hidden waterways can often be found in place names such as 'bridge', 'brook', 'bourne', 'water lane' and 'watergate'. Elements of ancient place names such as the Old English words *aewell* (river source), *burna* (stream) and *bece* (stream in a valley) can also act as pointers. Sometimes the very twists and turns of the road can betray the curves of an old forgotten river below. Keep an eye out for the signs and you'll be paying tribute to our lost waterways.

Wishing Well

The well in the garden of the cottage where I live is at least 55 feet deep. As our village had strong links with the medieval Knights Templar, I sometimes wonder if any treasure lies submerged at the bottom.

Perhaps because they were once literally life-giving sources, wells are often linked with ancient deities, saints and a sense of the holy. Even today you can find cloutie wells dotted around Britain and Ireland, visited by those who wish to say a healing prayer and then tie a piece of ribbon or cloth on a nearby tree as a sort of votive offering. There is something quite moving about the sight of dozens of little ribbons fluttering in the breeze like colourful fraying hopes.

For many of us, wells and ornamental fountains are open invitations to toss in a coin and make a wish. Yet the sight of the coin sinking to the bottom often makes me feel a strange mix of emotions – a sort of awkward optimism. When you next have the opportunity, spin a coin into a wishing well or fountain and have a think about what it is that you are wishing for.

The Sea, the Sea

The old music-hall song goes, 'Oh! I do like to be beside the seaside' – and most of us do indeed like to be beside the sea. Wealthy Romans enjoyed relaxing at the coast nearly two thousand years ago; however, it wasn't until the spread of railways in the mid-1800s that hoi polloi could afford to visit seaside resorts and promenade along the front.

The health benefits of being by the sea have been described by many – from the positive effects of the air's negative ions to the healing mineral salts in sea water. Being at the seaside is believed to strengthen the immune system and relax the mind and body. A 2012 study by the University of Exeter found that people who live close to the sea do tend to be healthier than those who are landlocked, with the benefits being felt most by those in less affluent coastal communities. Similarly, a study by Michigan State University found that people living close to the sea tend to be happier. Blue spaces, it seems, are as important for our health and happiness as green ones.

If you are unable to travel to the sea, let it come to you. Find a recording of the sound of waves crashing and play it while you lie back and close your eyes. Imagine the sea and that endless horizon. Let your mind drift with the ebb of the water . . .

Crabbing

Crabs are fascinating creatures that can be found in all the world's oceans, in fresh water and even on land. These blue-blooded decapods can grow back any limbs they lose, while their compound eyes are able to look in multiple directions at the same time.

Yet they're still quite easy to catch. If you'd like to go crabbing, fill a bucket with saltwater, a few pebbles and seaweed, and find a suitable spot along a harbour wall or pier. Then tie a piece of bait to a string or hand line. (No need for a hook.) Crabs are especially partial to bacon and fish.

Now sink your line in the water and wait for a crab to come calling. If you raise your line after a few minutes and it feels heavier, you might well find one or two tucking into your bait.

A net is useful for transferring crabs to the bucket, where you can take a close look at them. If you want to observe their crabby ways, keep the bucket in the shade with only a few crabs in it at a time and change the seawater every hour. In any case, don't keep these crustaceans in the bucket all day long, and if any start fighting, release them into the water's edge away from interested seagulls.

To pick one up, avoid the claws and hold the crab on either side of its shell or with one finger on top and one underneath – and handle with care. I once watched a young girl get a nasty surprise when she started poking at a large crab in a bucket. Much hand waving and wailing ensued before the crab finally let go of her finger and plopped serenely back into the sea.

The Simplicity of Shells

I'm not sure exactly what it is about seashells that makes them so beautiful – perhaps their muted colours, the perfection of their whorls, striations and ridges, the occasional glint of mother-of-pearl or how their chalky surfaces feel to the touch. On my desk there's a small glass bowl of shells that I've collected over the years, and whenever I look at them I'm reminded of happy times by the sea.

The study of shells is known as 'conchology', and our fascination with them dates back to the Stone Age, with shell jewellery having been found at ancient sites from China to Mexico. Shells – cowrie shells in particular – were also widely used as a form of currency. In addition to their scientific nomenclature, many types of shell have evocative names such as 'baby's ear', 'slipper shell', 'kitten's paw' and 'rose petal tellin', showing how they have captured our imaginations.

If you find an empty shell that appeals to you in some way, bring it home, rinse it clean, and draw or trace it. Shade in its patterns and colours. If you'd like to find out more about its former occupant, research your shell online or look it up in a shell identification guide.

––––– ∞ –––––

'You never enjoy the world aright, till the Sea itself floweth in your veins, till you are clothed with the heavens, and crowned with the stars . . .'

THOMAS TRAHERNE (1636–1674), *Centuries of Meditations*

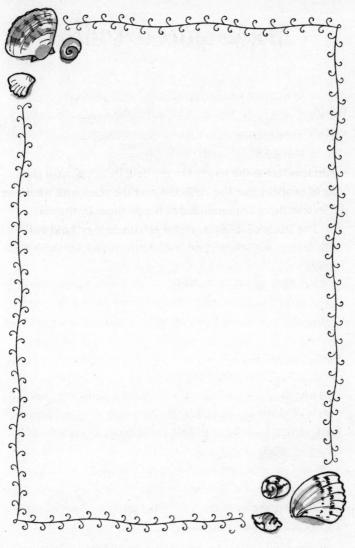

Shell found at _____

on _____

WATER

Drip or Dribble Castles

If you ever made sandcastles as a kid with a bucket and spade, you'll know the results can be a bit predictable and, well, bucket-shaped. For a more free-range, organic creation, try your hand at a dribble castle.

If you're at the seaside, dig a hole in the damp sand near the tidemark, but not so near that your castle will be washed away. When the hole's deep enough, it will fill with water: this is going to be your wet-sand quarry. If you're not at the beach, just fill a bucket with sand and cover the sand with water.

First, make a firm mound for your castle's foundations. Now start building onto the mound using handfuls of the waterlogged sand from your quarry or bucket. Take a fistful of wet sand (also known as sand mud or slurry) and let it dribble down slowly from your fist to form stalagmites. Keep on building, letting the sand trickle down into blobby towers and turrets, until you reach the height you want to achieve. If you really want to impress by creating archways and bridges, for instance, build your dribble castle upon an underlying structure made of sticks and stones.

While the exact provenance of dribble castles is uncertain, Gaudí's church, the Sagrada Família in Barcelona, gives the distinct impression that the architect might well have been an expert dribble-castle builder.

Rock Pooling

Once or twice I've gone beachcombing and picked up a large shell along the shoreline, only to find it inhabited by a hermit crab – always an unexpected pleasure. I've carefully returned the crab to where I found it.

Depending on the geography of the coastline, if you venture along the seafront at low tide, you might well come across rock pools teeming with creatures. Peer into pools to look for shrimp and prawns, crabs, sea anemones and small fish. A net might harm some of the more delicate creatures, so lift pebbles and part seaweed with your hands. If you're lucky, you might even discover a starfish.

Leaving the creatures where they are, bring that sense of curiosity back home with you. Where there's water there's life, and this is true in the most surprising of places; I once spotted newts lying camouflaged in a puddle at the heart of the woods. Wherever you are, keep looking beyond the surface – and who knows what you might find?

Wood

ouch wood, the saying goes, to ward off bad luck. In folk tales, woods are often magical places in which transformations take place. Today, they provide breathing spaces and habitats in which animals and plants can thrive and interact freely. Professor Suzanne Simard of the University of British Columbia has shown how trees can communicate with each other, with 'mother' trees acting as hubs in hidden forest networks.

When felled, wood is an immensely versatile material, providing fuel, shelter and much more. Discover the beauty of wood yourself by walking peacefully among the trees, carving a spoon or making your own charcoal. Cook up an elderflower cordial or go nutting. Climb a tree and try to catch a spinning leaf.

Touch wood to rekindle your creative fire.

'Of all the works of the creation which know the changes of life and death, the trees of the forest have the longest existence.'

SUSAN FENIMORE COOPER (1813–1894), *Rural Hours*

Shinrin-yoku, or Forest Bathing

Shinrin-yoku is a simple yet powerful practice. It started in Japan in the 1980s and has become a key part of the country's preventative health care. Over the years, various studies have shown its many benefits – from reducing blood pressure to increasing energy levels and NK cell counts (NKs, or natural killer cells, are associated with a strong immune system and cancer prevention).

Today, *Shinrin-yoku* is better known in the West as 'forest bathing' or 'forest therapy'.

Happily, forest bathing doesn't mean rolling about naked in a sea of pine needles (although that might be interesting). All it entails is a gentle walk among the trees.

Before you embark on your woodland walk, set your intention: to simply be, meandering at leisure without worrying about your destination or how many steps you've taken that day.

Settle down for a moment, quietly, under a canopy of green leaves, breathing in deeply, and watch the shadows dapple around you . . .

—— ∞ ——

*'The clearest way into the Universe is through
a forest wilderness.'*

John Muir (1838–1914), *John of the Mountains*

Climb a Tree

Some time ago I was out walking in the woods with friends, one of whom had recovered from a serious illness. This friend suddenly launched himself at an oak tree and climbed high up into its boughs. His two children clambered up after him and soon they were all perched there, laughing down at the rest of us. Having survived his illness and re-evaluated his approach to life, my friend was set for adventure – and here was one readily at hand, up in the forest canopy.

Now, I have done a bit of tree climbing myself and it hasn't always gone well – like the time I missed my footing and fell waist-deep into a stream. But if you do manage to get up into the branches without incident, it's an immensely satisfying feeling: literally a fresh perspective on the world from up among the leaves.

The trick is to overcome any feeling of fear or apprehension and find those first handholds and footholds. Then feel your way up steadily, one movement at a time, making full use of your body – fingers, toes, arms, legs, backside – while shifting your weight carefully. And remember that it's often harder to come down, as you can't always see where you're going, so be sure to remember the way and perhaps take a companion with you when you first go climbing, just in case.

Whistle in the Woods

'May whistles' were traditionally made in Cornwall on the first day of May to celebrate the arrival of summer. The whistle is usually made from the sap-rich shoot of a sycamore tree – a member of the maple genus with a five-pointed leaf – and will work until the wood dries out. You will need:

* A sharp knife (blunt knives are dangerous for carving).
* A straight twig of sycamore – ash or willow will work fine as well – about 15 cm (6 in) long and 1 cm (just under ½ in) thick, cut from the tree with a knife in the spring or early summer.

Cut an angular nick off the top of the twig to create a mouthpiece. (Think of the shape of a recorder.)

From the top, measure about 10 cm (4 in) down the twig and score a circle round the outer bark.

Using the handle of your knife or another piece of wood, tap along the bark of the whistle's top section, from the mouthpiece down to the score mark. This releases the sap underneath.

On either side of the circular cut, twist firmly in opposite directions. Carefully slide the tube of bark off the top section, then slip it back into place.

About 1.5 cm (½ in) from the top, cut a deep V-shaped notch through the outer bark into the wood below. This will be where the sound comes out.

Slide off the top bark again, and keep this safe.

From below the V-shaped notch, hollow out a flat sound chamber as deep as the notch and about 3 cm (1¼ in) long.

Cut a thin layer of wood from the whistle's mouthpiece down to the chamber to create a channel for air.

Slide the tube of bark back into place to seal the whistle – and blow!

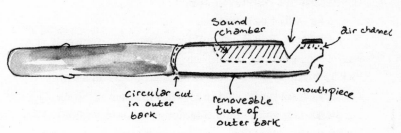

WOOD

Elderflower Magic

White, frothy and pungent, elderflowers mark the start
of summer. The elder shrub – it's barely a tree – grows in
urban wastelands and country hedgerows, and its florets
make a fine cordial or champagne. It's a plant with strong
magical associations in folklore, so – being a slightly
superstitious sort – I tend to ask permission from the
tree before taking anything from it.

Elderflower Cordial

75 elderflower heads
50 g (2 oz) citric acid
4 oranges, roughly chopped
4 lemons, roughly chopped
2 kg (4 lb 4 oz) sugar
4.5 litres (160 fl oz) boiling water

Pick approximately 75 white elderflower heads on a sunny
day, away from traffic, and use them straightaway. Shake
out any insects and put the elderflower heads in a sterilised
bucket or very large pan. (All your equipment for this recipe
should be sterilised, including the bottles.)

Add the citric acid, the oranges and lemons to the bucket,
along with the sugar. Pour the boiling water over the
ingredients, stir well and cover.

Leave to cool overnight and stir two or three more times before straining the syrupy cordial through muslin into another large saucepan or bucket. Then pour into bottles using a funnel.

Don't completely fill the bottles so as to allow enough room for gas, should the cordial begin to ferment and fizz. The cordial will last for about a week in the fridge, but can be frozen in three-quarters-full plastic bottles.

Serve diluted with water and ice to taste, perhaps with a dash of lemon, and enjoy the taste of summer in a glass.

—— ∞ ——

'... there is a Spirit in the woods.'

WILLIAM WORDSWORTH (1770–1850), 'Nutting'

Welcome to the Insect Hotel

If you'd like to invite more beneficial insects such as bees and ladybirds into your neighbourhood, why not create your own insect hotel?

At its simplest, all you'll need are a few hollow bamboo canes and a piece of string. Cut the bamboo to lengths of about 15 cm (6 in), tie them together tightly and hang the bundle about 1.5 metres (5 feet) up in a sunny and sheltered spot. With time, solitary bees may use the bundle as a nesting site, sealing up the entrances to create little chambers.

For a better-furnished hotel, fill a lidless wooden box or an open-fronted bird house with separate sections of very tightly packed bamboo canes, twigs and pine cones, as well as seed heads or lichen. Fix the box outdoors, so the canes lie horizontally. Aphid-eating ladybirds will hibernate among the twigs and in the bamboo hollows, while spiders and insects such as beetles and woodlice might well move in beside them. (I'm afraid there's little you can do to ensure they all get along and don't start eating each other.)

If you want to build the Ritz of insect hotels, stack up layers of pallets and fill the gaps with dead wood, dry leaves, straw and hay, rolled-up cardboard, logs and old carpet, as well as the usual bundles of bamboo or reeds. For fine dining, add some elderberry, rose and blackberry shoots for your guests to munch. Luxury.

Carve Your Own Spoon

There is something very rewarding about carving your own spoon, as – with practice – the results can be as pleasing as they are practical. To make this basic spoon, you will need:

* A piece of green wood (i.e. wood that is unseasoned or newly cut) approximately 20 cm (8 in) long, with a diameter of about 6 cm (2½ in). Alder, apple, lime, birch and cherry work particularly well, as these are easier to carve.
* A very sharp knife, such as a bushcraft knife. (Never use a blunt knife or a folding knife with a blade you can't lock open.)
* A pencil or piece of charcoal.
* Medium-coarse sandpaper and horse-grade linseed oil or nut oil (optional).

Remove the bark from the branch by peeling, stripping and whittling it off. Carve away from your body, using small, economical movements.

Working on a stable surface, split the wood along its length so the soft pith at its core sits at the top of the piece you're going to work. This will leave the wood's natural curvature below for the spoon's bowl. To split the wood, place the edge of your knife on the round end of the wood and, being careful not to slip or to get your knife stuck, use another offcut as a mallet to knock the knife into the wood until the length splits in two. Turn the blade slightly to follow the core as you go. Discard one of the pieces.

On the piece you want to use for your spoon, sketch your design on the flat surface with a pencil or charcoal. Mark the outlines of the handle and the outer bowl. (If you like, use a kitchen spoon as a template.)

Begin to carve around the outline, following the direction of the wood grain as best you can and working from both ends, remembering it's a three-dimensional object. Chamfer the top two corners of the bowl so you end up with a chunky lollipop shape.

Draw the spoon's inner bowl. For this next tricky stage, it's best to use a knife with a relatively short yet sturdy blade, or a special spoon gouge. Stab your knife into the bowl's centre, then very carefully and slowly gouge out a dimple from where you can begin to scoop out the rest, working across the grain and down into the bottom of the bowl. Take your time, to avoid slipping and cutting yourself or making errors. The bowl shouldn't be too deep, as this won't be comfortable to eat with.

Once the bowl is hollowed out, go back over the rest of the spoon, trimming down the handle and working on the profile, to give you a comfortable grip when you round off the outside of the bowl.

Smooth the spoon's surface by running the knife gently over it, perhaps even using the knife's spine at this stage. Store the spoon at room temperature for a day or two to let the wood dry a little, then sandpaper it.

If you wish, coat your spoon with two or three layers of horse-grade linseed oil (not normal woodwork linseed) or nut oil, which will enhance the grain and protect the wood, preventing it from splitting. Allow 24 hours between coats.

Now sit back and admire your handiwork.

Catch a Falling Leaf

As a child, I remember scores of children flocking under the chestnut trees in autumn to catch the falling leaves for luck. Leaf catching was considerably more exciting than sports day and – it turns out – an older tradition.

There are various superstitions about catching leaves. One is that if you catch a leaf on the first day of autumn, you'll remain free from colds for the following year. Some believe you'll have a lucky month for each leaf you catch, while others say you should make a wish if you catch a leaf, then keep the leaf safe during the winter until the first green buds appear in spring.

Personally, I like the idea that catching a falling leaf is somehow lucky, pure and simple. On a blustery autumn day, I still try to catch them – it's especially fun to do with family and friends. In our household, leaf catching can get very competitive, as it's much more difficult to do than you might think.

Have a go and see how you get on. If you succeed, you could keep your leaf in your pocket till, dried out and fragile, it crumbles. (My coat pockets are full of leaf crumb.) Or tape it here in your journal for safekeeping – a seasonal reminder that to achieve some things in life, all you need are a little skill and a measure of luck.

Leaf caught on _____

at _____

Conkers

Conkers is an excellent game won by smashing your opponent's weapon to pieces. To prepare your conker, you will need:

* A conker: the shiny seed of the horse chestnut tree with its spiny outer casement removed.
* A tool to bore a small, round hole in the conker: a small screwdriver, drill, skewer or penknife will do.
* A piece of string, twine or bootlace about 20 cm (8 in) long.

Let your conker harden in a dry place for a day or two. (Some people cheat by using last year's rock-hard conkers, or by soaking them in vinegar or baking them.) Make a hole through the conker with your tool. Tie a granny knot in the string and thread the other end through the hole so the conker hangs securely from the string.

To play, one player dangles their conker by the top of the string for their opponent to swing at and hit. If the opponent misses, the two players swap places. If the strings become tangled, the first player to shout 'Strings!' gets a free strike. If a player's conker falls on the ground, the other can shout 'Stamps!' and stamp on it. To protect the fallen conker, the other player must shout 'No stamps!' before the would-be conker-crusher can call out.

A conker earns points for each opponent it annihilates, and if it defeats another champion it wins all that conker's points too. If, for example, you were to smash an opponent's 'nine-er' (a conker with nine scalps to its name) with a new conker, your victorious conker would automatically become a 'tenner'!

It's a brutal business.

——— ∞ ———

'For luck you carried a horse chestnut and a rabbit's foot in your right pocket.'

ERNEST HEMINGWAY (1899–1961),
A Moveable Feast

Colour Wheel

Andy Goldsworthy (b. 1956) is an artist who works with nature to make his creations. His art installations are not built to last, but are made from materials such as leaves, sand, ice, flowers and feathers that are carefully laid out in patterns. He doesn't use manmade materials, but prefers the designs to hold themselves together through natural tensions. The artworks are site specific and are meant to be ephemeral. He photographs them to record them.

Andy Goldsworthy's artwork *Rowan Leaves and Hole* (1987) is the inspiration here. In it, he has laid out a circular band of rowan leaves around a hole. The band is dark at the outside, but the colours become brighter towards the centre, moving through crimsons, reds, oranges and yellows around the black hole at the circle's heart.

Make your own leaf art by collecting leaves of different colours and hues. Lay them out in patterns that please you.

A simple yet beautiful way to start might be to create your own colour wheel, going from deep, dark shades such as black, browns and purples, through to vivid greens and bright yellows.

Create your art in a spot outdoors, for someone else to find. Or dry the leaves out and stick them to a card to keep.

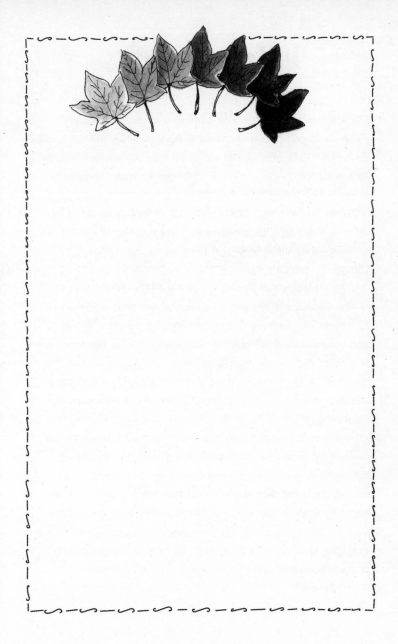

WOOD

Hedging Your Bets

Other than being baffled by them in a maze, it's unlikely many of us pay much attention to hedges. They might seem little more than boundaries or obstacles – in-between spaces of limited interest. Yet some hedges can be many hundreds of years old, going back to medieval times and beyond.

In his book *Hedges* (1974), Dr Max Hooper came up with a rule for dating a hedge, based on the number of woody species – excluding ivy – that have colonised a 27-metre (30-yard) stretch:

Age = number of woody species × 110 + 30 years.

Why not apply Hooper's rule when you next come across an interesting-looking hedgerow? Pace along it for 30 yards and count the woody plants, such as ash, beech, blackthorn, brambles, elder, field maple, hawthorn, hazel, holly, oak, sycamore and willow. Write down your findings, make your calculation and, if possible, check it against old maps in the local library.

Hooper's rule has been widely disputed and doesn't work for hedges more than a thousand years old, such as those dating back to the Bronze and Iron Ages. Nor does it take into account the fact that some hedges might not have been single species or 'pure' when they were originally planted; they might have included elm or other useful timber trees, for example. However, he does invite us to give hedges their due as the fascinating and historically important habitats that they are.

Acorn Coffee

The saying goes that 'Mighty oaks from little acorns grow', but there's a lot to recommend the humble acorn on its own merits. While acorns taste bitter if eaten raw because of the tannins they contain, they make a fine drink and were used as a substitute for coffee during the Second World War. Raw acorns can be stored in a cool, dark place for months before using.

To make acorn coffee, pick about half a kilo or 1lb of ripe nut-brown acorns, ignoring any that are green or black. Remove the cupules – the little cups at the base – then boil the acorns in their shells for 15–20 minutes until the water turns dark brown. (If you want to make sure they are completely leached/blanched, pour off the water and repeat the process until the water stays clear.) Drain and let them cool before peeling off their outer shells. Cut the kernels in half and spread them out on a baking tray somewhere warm for a day or two to dry them out.

Chop up the kernels and grind the pieces in a coffee grinder or with a pestle and mortar. To get fine granules, sieve and regrind any lumpy bits. (Acorn flour is made this way too, but with even more sieving and grinding to remove the fibres.) Once you have your granules, spread them over a baking tray and grill for a few minutes until dark brown, making sure they don't burn.

To make a hot drink, use one teaspoon of granules per cup of boiling water, steep for a couple of minutes and strain if necessary into another cup. Add milk and sugar to taste, or let it cool and drink cold with a drop of honey.

WOOD

Stripping the Willow

Willow is a tree as versatile as it is beautiful. In winter, knotted willow trees blaze like orange crowns in the landscape; in summer, weeping willows lean over waterways as if dreaming of their own reflections. Willow bark and leaves were used for pain relief in the ancient Near East and by Native Americans; and an extract of the bark called salicin is the precursor of aspirin. Moreover, the plant's pliable shoots can be turned into wicker and woven into basketwork. And it makes a fine drawing charcoal.

To create your own drawing charcoal, cut one or two withies of willow and strip them clean with a potato peeler. (You could also use the woody shoots of a grapevine.) Snip the shoots into sticks the width of your palm, and bundle several together. Wrap the bundle tightly in two layers of kitchen foil, followed by two looser protective layers. Place the bundle on the glowing embers of a barbeque or fireplace for anything from a couple of hours to overnight, depending on the thickness of the sticks and the heat of the embers. Remove the baked bundle and let it cool completely before unwrapping – to reveal your charcoal sticks. If they're not quite done, wrap them up again and put them back on the heat till they're ready.

This process might take a couple of test trials, so experiment and see what works for you. (You could even try baking foil-wrapped willow in the oven.) When you've achieved the results you want, remember how you got there; then draw to your heart's content with your homemade charcoal.

———— ∞ ————

'Trees are sanctuaries. Whoever knows how to speak to them, whoever knows how to listen to them, can learn the truth.'

HERMANN HESSE (1877–1962), *Trees: Reflections and Poems*

Barking

If you've made your own charcoal, you could use it to create a bark rubbing. All you'll need are a sheet of paper and a drawing medium such as your charcoal, a soft pencil, pastels or wax crayons. And a tree.

Press your paper against the tree's bark and rub your charcoal stick or crayon over it until the pattern and texture of the bark comes through. If you have a couple of different colour crayons or pastels with you, use these to create contrasting layers. And, while you're there, take a moment or two to enjoy the feel of the bark under your hands.

Turn the results into an abstract piece of art or cut up the rubbing to make a collage; or stick them in the space opposite – whatever appeals to you.

Different types of tree have different patterned bark, so if you're unsure what species of tree you've been leaning up against, you might be able to identify it by comparing your bark rubbing with the images in a field guide.

Swing Time

If you've ever come across a rope swing in the woods, you'll know it's hard to resist having a go. To make your own, you'll need:

* A piece of strong, durable rope about 2 cm (¾ in) thick, long enough to be tied over the bough and attached to a piece of branch at one end.
* A tree growing above a soft landing site, with a healthy bough about 2.5 metres (8 feet) off the ground. The diameter of the bough should be at least 20 cm (8 in).
* A piece of sturdy fallen branch about 40 cm (16 in) long and 4 cm (1½ in) thick, to act as a seat.

Make a sliding loop at one end of the rope using a running bowline knot or a slip knot. (If you don't know how to make these, just tie a loop as best and as tightly as you can.) Then throw the other end of the rope over the bough. If necessary, you can tie a smaller bit of wood to the end to act as a weight as you throw it. Once it's over, pull the end back through the loop and tug on it to secure the rope to the bough.

Tie the dangling end of the rope to the middle of the piece of branch at a height of about 60 cm (24 in) above the ground.

Now take a seat and gently swing . . .

How to Wield an Axe

There are various ways to wield an axe depending on whether you want to chop down redwoods or simply split logs. Here's how to use an axe to make firewood.

First, pull on a pair of sturdy boots and ensure the area around you is clear of anything that might cause you to lose your footing or catch the axe's blade when you swing it. For firewood and kindling, use an axe with a relatively short handle of approximately 35 cm (13½ in).

Place the piece of wood you want to split vertically on a chopping block or level ground, with any knots in the wood towards the bottom of the piece. With your feet set slightly wider apart than your shoulders and with soft knees, position yourself where you can swing at the centre of the wood with straight arms.

Hold the axe firmly but not too tightly with both hands towards the bottom of the handle. Then look directly at where you plan to strike and, using your elbow joint as a fulcrum, pull the axe back so it swings up past you on one side. When the axe reaches the top of its arc, allow it to fall back down, guiding it to where you want to cut. Split the log in half, then quarters. If it helps, roar like a Viking.

———— ∞ ————

'Time spent in sharpening the axe may well be spared from swinging it.'

JOSIAH STRONG (1847–1916), *The Times and Young Men*

Stumped

Glimpsed in the forest, ancient tree stumps sit squat and burly as gnome kings cloaked in moss. While they might have fallen from their glory days, they provide valuable habitats for all sorts of life, from fungi, insects and reptiles to birds and small mammals.

To age the stump of a recently felled tree, count the growth rings on the horizontal cross-section of its trunk. In countries with warm summers and cold winters, trees generally form one growth ring a year; in spring, the wood grows quickly and looks lighter, whereas summer growth tends to be slower, resulting in denser, darker wood. To find out how many years old the tree is, count the number of dark rings. (The different growing conditions in, for example, tropical climates mean that tree-ring dating can't be done there in quite the same way.)

The rings will also tell you about the tree's life as a whole, with wide rings revealing good growing seasons and narrower rings suggesting drier or colder years, as well as whether anything has leant against the tree or otherwise prevented it from growing.

To create a snapshot of a tree's life – and of history – photograph the rings on a tree stump and match them to specific years. That way, you'll not only learn about the tree, but gain insights into the conditions in which it has grown over the decades.

Around the Fire

The last rays of light have faded and there's a chill in the air. But it doesn't matter: it's snug by the fire, lit by the glow of the flames . . .

There's something primitive yet romantic about a campfire. To make one of your own, dig a small, shallow fire pit in a safe spot away from trees and bushes or anything that might be set alight. Then edge the pit with rocks to stop people stumbling into it and to prevent burning wood falling out.

In the middle of the pit, make a small pile of kindling with dry twigs and grass, crisp leaves and perhaps a piece or two of cardboard or balled-up paper (making sure this can't blow away once the fire is lit). Over the kindling, construct a tepee from larger pieces of wood.

Lean in and light the kindling in one or two places to get the fire going. If necessary, blow on the embers to help spark them into life. Once the fire is burning, add larger pieces of wood to feed the flames. Then settle in the warmth. When the fire has burnt down, skewer a marshmallow or two on a long, thin stick and toast them over the hot embers, turning them for a few minutes till they're crisp and golden on the outside, gooey in the centre – a small yet perfect pleasure.

Feather

A feather might be soft and light, barely a tickle against the palm, yet strong enough to carry a bird many thousands of miles. While feathers protect birds against the elements, keeping them warm and dry, they also help them to communicate or camouflage themselves. They're an evolutionary wonder.

'Hope is the thing with feathers / That perches in the soul,' wrote the poet Emily Dickinson. There is something truly uplifting about the sight of birds flying across the horizon – as though they know no limits and are not even bound by gravity.

Enjoy a taste of their freedom. Wake up with the dawn chorus and study the language of birds. Build a nest box and welcome the sounds of the hedgerows and summer skies into your life. Make a quill pen, then write a song of your own. Dare to fly . . .

— ∞ —

'I hope you love birds too. It is economical.
It saves going to heaven.'

EMILY DICKINSON (1830–1886), *Letters, Vol. 1*

FEATHER

Feather Light

Find a feather – any kind will do. Hold the quill and run your finger along the up-curved edge, noticing how the vane flexes under your touch. Perhaps the barbs separate and then rejoin.

When some birds preen, they secrete preen oil from their uropygial gland, which they spread onto their feathers using their beaks and feet to help keep the feathers waterproof. Birds such as owls, hawks and pigeons don't have this type of gland but have specialised feathers that disintegrate into powder down, which serves the same purpose as the oil.

Trace or sketch your feather on the page opposite here. Colour it in.

If you want to, label its anatomy, such as the vanes on either side, the after feathers (towards the feather's base), rachis (spine down the middle) and barbs (the branches off the rachis).

Can you identify the bird it belongs to?

The Eurasian jay has startling patches of beautiful, tiny, bright blue feathers on its wings. When I'm lucky and my eyes are particularly sharp, I can sometimes find one of these feathers hidden among the leaf litter like a tiny jewel while I'm out walking in the woods.

Feather found on _____

F E A T H E R

Write Like Shakespeare

If you fancy writing with a Shakespearean flourish, start by making your own quill pen. Birds naturally shed damaged feathers, so you might find a suitable feather on the ground where large waterfowl such as swans or geese have been waddling about. If you live in a city, park ponds are a good place to look.

To make your quill you will need:

* A feather
* A sharp craft knife
* Tweezers/a straightened paper clip
* A pot of ink

First, select your feather, which should be long enough to hold comfortably and have a sturdy shaft, thick enough to hold ink.

Grip the feather as you would a pen, following the feather's natural curve so the point curves downward. You want your quill's nib to point in this direction.

Lie the feather flat and, with a sharp craft knife or your fingers, trim the side that will sit above your hand – the after feathers and some of the barbs – to leave more room for a better grip.

Next, gently scrape the extra scale off the tip of the quill to make it smooth and even.

With your knife, cut the end of the quill at an angle less than 45 degrees.

Clean out any dried membrane from inside the cut shaft with tweezers or with something wiry like a straightened paper clip.

Now cut off the very tip of the quill to leave a flat end.

Carve off slivers down both sides of your new nib to give it a slightly sharper profile similar to the V-shaped point of a fountain-pen nib, but keeping the end blunt.

Dip the nib in a little ink and try it out. Trim it a little more if necessary.

Now you're all set to pen a masterpiece . . .

Wake Up with the Dawn Chorus

A chorus of birdsong makes for a beautiful start to the day, although you'll have to be an early riser to catch the best of it in spring and summer. In the UK, the dawn chorus can start as early as 3 a.m. when the sky begins to brighten slightly in summer. Blackbirds are usually the first to sing, followed by robins, wrens, thrushes, finches and those late-risers the hedge sparrows. The earlier birds like eating worms, which can be found above ground at first light, whereas those who join in later tend to prefer insects or seeds.

In the USA, there are over 400 species of songbirds and each region has its own unique sound – with distinct regional accents in species such as the cardinals. There are also regional differences in the dawn chorus in Australia, where the territory ranges from wet eucalypt forests to dry bush.

However, the choir in all dawn choruses is typically male, with each member proclaiming his territory to females in a bid to attract a mate, and to warn off potential rivals. The chill, calm morning air allows the sound of their song to travel up to 20 times further than at noon.

If you'd like to treat yourself to a free sound-bath, just immerse yourself in birdsong. Pour yourself a mug of hot coffee and step outside in the early morning to listen. What can you hear? Jot down your findings, and, if you enjoy the experience, compare choruses on different days, or record them. (There is a theory that birdsong has actually got louder in the last 50 years to overcome traffic noise.) With time, you might even get to know your soloists.

Bird Language

Besides singing, birds make a range of different noises. Once you've tuned in to the birdsong in your area, why not create your own dictionary of bird language?

Start by listing the other sounds you hear them make, which might fall into one of the following types:

Alarm calls: often short, loud and repeated bursts of noise, useful for telling if a predator such as a cat or hawk is in the area. The blackbird has a very distinctive chink-chink-chink alarm call, while the tiny wren makes a loud tek-tek-tek noise.

Begging calls: peeps and tweets made by juvenile birds to attract a parent's attention, often with wing flutters. You might well spot the parent nearby, looking suitably frazzled.

Contact calls: such as the chirps made by a family of long-tailed tits, letting each other know where they are and whether they've found a source of food, or the flight calls of a skein of geese as they migrate overhead.

Keep an ear out for non-vocal bird noises too, such as bill drumming and snapping. Then move on to postural displays such as bowing, drooping the wings or fanning the tail. What might these mean from a bird's perspective?

—— ∞ ——

'The air is crowded with birds – beautiful, tender, intelligent birds – to whom life is a song.'

GEORGE HENRY LEWES (1817–1878), *Studies in Animal Life*

Make Your Own Bird Feeder

I love watching the birds in our garden. Regular visitors include robins, blackbirds, finches and wrens, and there's a woodpecker who arrives whenever I put out a particular upmarket bird food that he likes. In the spring, a pair of loved-up woodpigeons regularly turn up to snack on birdseed before strutting their stuff on the pergola. (I don't know – pigeons, using the place like a cheap hotel.)

It's easy, of course, to buy bird feeders. But you could make your own. Just cut an oblong hole in the side of a clean, empty plastic drinks bottle, sealed at the top. Make sure the hole is large enough to allow birds to reach the food inside, but not so big that it'll all fall out. Pierce the bottom of the bottle a couple of times to allow rainwater to drain away. Then fill the bottle with good-quality bird seed (if you have a nut allergy, don't use food that contains nuts), and hang up the feeder with string or wire where the birds can reach it safely.

Alternatively, fill it with a homemade bird fat ball. To make this, mash together raisins, peanuts (if you're not allergic), bird seed and grated cheese with a large dollop of softened lard or suet. When the ingredients hold together, shape the mixture into a ball and place in your feeder. If the food becomes mouldy, clean it out and replace it with fresh supplies. Once the birds get used to you feeding them, they'll begin to rely on you as a food source and keep returning. All the better to get to know them.

Pecking Orders

Pecking orders were first spotted among domestic hens but have been found in studies of flocks of wild birds too. According to the pecking order – or 'dominance hierarchy', to use the correct lingo – an alpha bird will peck any other bird in the flock, whereas a beta bird will peck all of them apart from the alpha bird. Male birds tend to be dominant over females, while adults rank higher than younger birds. But, like any hierarchy, the power can shift as the group dynamic changes.

If you have your own birdfeeder, find out whether there's a pecking order among the birds that visit it. Do any of the birds wait respectfully for their turn, or do they chase each other off? Perhaps a particular individual rules the roost? Our garden is occasionally visited by a clattering of jackdaws, and it's interesting to see which of them will act as lookouts while the others go in to feed.

Sometimes, of course, avian delusions of grandeur can come spectacularly unstuck. One autumn, a pheasant in a nearby village decided to make the whole lane his territory, and took to attacking a particular woman whenever she dared to walk down it. Perhaps unsurprisingly, his behaviour didn't win him friends and he soon came to a sticky end.

You're on the List

Serious birdwatchers, or twitchers, are often keen listers. This might mean keeping a list of all the species they've seen at home or abroad. Some, however, make annual lists of birds spotted during a particular year, while others might start separate lists of birds seen in different counties, states or countries. It can get rather competitive, a bit like catching the collecting bug. There are even league tables of champion listers, some of whom manage to tick off over 9,000 different species – an amazing feat.

While I'm not a lister, I jot a line in my diary whenever I see a bird that captures my imagination in some way. This might be something as obvious as sighting the first swallow in spring or the crimson flash of a bullfinch disappearing over a hedge. And I was enchanted to watch my first hummingbirds close up during a visit to Tennessee, their wings an emerald blur as they sipped on a feeder hanging in the porch.

Start to note down the different types of birds you spot, along with a short line about the significance of that sighting for you. Alongside this list, draw up a wish list: are there any birds that would make your day if you came across them, and where in the world might you find them?

DIY Nest Box

If you have the space outdoors, why not put up a nest box? Either buy one or, if you fancy a DIY project, make your own.

You will need:

* A plank of untreated wood, ideally 15 mm thick, 150 mm wide and 130 cm long (approximately 0.6 × 6 × 51 in) to allow a little room for error.
* A tape measure and pencil for marking out.
* A handsaw.
* Sandpaper.
* A drill.
* A flat drill bit for making the nest-box entry hole. A 32 mm (1¼ in) flat drill bit will make the right sized hole for attracting house sparrows, whereas blue, coal and marsh tits prefer 25 mm (1 in).
* An 8 mm (⅓ in) drill bit.
* A hammer and twenty 2.5 cm (1 in) galvanised nails.
* A strip of waterproof rubber 220 mm (8½ in) long and 80 mm (3 in) wide (e.g. cut from a bicycle inner tube or butyl rubber), to create the hinge for the lid.
* Enough plastic-coated wire to secure the box into place outside.

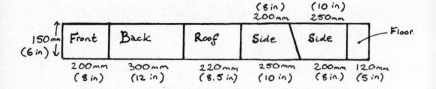

Mark the plank into the sections below, and cut them with the saw.

Sand all rough edges to protect the birds.

Use the flat wood drill bit to drill the hole in the front panel. Position the hole about 125 mm (approximately 5 in) up from the base of the box, so the nestlings can't fall out. (If you'd like to attract larger birds into your nest box, forget about the hole and simply saw the front section in half, leaving the top half of the front open.)

Drill two drainage holes in the base to let liquid waste drain away.

Assemble the box as shown opposite and nail it together, hammering gently to avoid splitting the wood. Make sure none of the nails pokes through into the nesting area. No need to paint or varnish the box, as the grain of the wood will enable the chicks to grip onto the surface.

To create a hinged lid, cut the rubber strip to the width of the box, then nail it to the back of the box and to the lid. (Or screw the lid loosely into place so you can remove it later.)

This will let you clean the box, but do keep the lid closed to stop predators such as magpies from raiding the nest.

Drill two small holes 50 mm (2 in) apart at the top on the back and thread the coated wire through them. Use the wire to tie your nest box securely in place. (Alternatively, attach it at the top with a screw.) Position it somewhere high up, away from predators and out of strong sunlight or wind.

Et voilà! Now you just have to hope your nest box meets with the approval of the local birds.

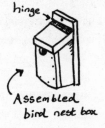

Assembled bird nest box

Open front for larger birds

A Song of Your Own

Throughout the ages, birds have inspired literature and the fine arts. In the twelfth century, the Persian poet Farid ud-Din Attar penned his Sufi masterpiece *The Conference of the Birds*, while John Keats wrote 'Ode to a Nightingale' in 1819 and Ted Hughes's powerful *Crow* sequence was published in 1970. Birds take poetic flight in many great works.

If you find yourself inspired by birds in some way – perhaps you're drawn to a particular species or are fascinated by their behaviour – why not explore this in writing? Should the idea of sitting down to write poetry make you uncomfortable, perhaps approach it as though you were piecing together song lyrics, or simply scribbling down a few thoughts that might be strung together at a later date.

I wrote the poem 'Night Blanket' after listening to a blackbird singing during the night. It's not long, it's not elaborate, yet I hope it shows how even a simple experience can inspire a piece of writing.

In the Notes section (see page 183), begin to jot down some thoughts of your own – words and phrases that could be the start of something longer.

'Night Blanket'

A blackbird is threading a song
through the blanket of the night;

bright notes embroider the dark
as I lie here, listening.

Such strange, delicate work
in this lonely hour,

each fluted phrase
tacks the edges of sleep.

Somewhere in the cold,
a blackbird refills its throat

and I pull the sound
around me.

A Mischief of Magpies

With their dramatic black-and-white plumage, magpies know how to make an entrance. These clever birds have a reputation as thieves and predators, and are often considered birds of ill omen. The nursery rhyme goes:

> One for sorrow,
> Two for joy,
> Three for a girl,
> Four for a boy,
> Five for silver,
> Six for gold,
> Seven for a secret never to be told.

It's worth bearing these numbers in mind should you spot a mischief of magpies and have enough time to count them. A family friend once failed an exam because she worked herself into a state when she spotted a solitary magpie through the window as she was turning over her paper – a self-fulfilling prophecy perhaps. If she'd had any sense, she'd have looked for another to bring joy, or quickly saluted it by saying 'Good morning, captain' and her bad luck would have been averted.

If you find a magpie wing or tail feather, hold it to the light and you will see its metallic sheen, shifting through greens, blues and purple to tinges of red – a hint that beauty can sometimes be found in the very tail of misfortune.

Living the High Life

As most farmers will tell you, if rooks are spotted strutting around a field it's a sure sign rain is on the way. Rooks are members of the Corvidae family, which includes crows, choughs, ravens, jackdaws, nutcrackers, jays and magpies. Although rooks have grey-white faces and pointed beaks, it can sometimes be difficult to tell them apart from carrion crows. However, they are more sociable birds: as the saying goes, 'A crow in a crowd is a rook, a rook on its own is a crow.'

In built-up areas, crows are more tolerant of company than out in the countryside, yet they still don't live in nesting colonies like rooks do. A busy rookery high up among the treetops is a fabulous sight; I used to be able to observe one at close quarters when I was a student and watched them fledging in spring – a fitting metaphor, I guess, for graduation. Although there were inevitably a couple of casualties.

If you are lucky enough to have a bird colony of some description near where you live, take a little time to get to know the residents and see the fascinating interactions of the birds at close hand. Keep a note of your findings.

Great Bird Spectacles

Great bird spectacles isn't a reference to fancy feathery eyewear but to the amazing avian gatherings that occur around the world. Among the best known in Europe and the USA are the murmurations that occur when huge flocks of starlings dive and swoop in unison, creating incredible pixelated patterns in the sky.

Not so acrobatic, yet still impressive, are migrating waxwings, which often arrive in great irruptions – the collective noun for these birds being a 'museum' or 'earful' – wherever there are berries they can feed on. One particularly harsh winter, they chased off the blackbirds from my neighbour's crab apple tree and filled its branches with their high-pitched trilling, curiously exotic with their red plumage and prominent crests.

Wherever you live, the likelihood is you won't have to travel far to come across an impressive spectacle of birds. These might be gulls breeding in seaside colonies, swifts gathering high over city centres or wagtails bobbing around a car park. If you have the opportunity, do a little research to find out about nearby avian gatherings and witness the wonder of them for yourself.

Birds of a Feather

There are some brilliantly evocative collective nouns for groups of birds. These include:

A bellowing of bullfinches	A murder of crows
A cast of falcons	A parliament of owls
A charm of finches	A pitying of turtledoves
A deceit of lapwings	A scold of jays
An exaltation of larks	A twack of ducks
A hedge of herons	A wake of buzzards

There's no rule, however, to say you can't add to these with collective nouns of your own. Spend a little time watching the birds on your windowsill, observing their behaviour and characteristics, and see if any words or descriptions strike you. What about a swoop of swallows, for example, or a squabble of sparrows?

Let your imagination fly.

───── ∞ ─────

'Birds of a feather will gather together.'

ROBERT BURTON (1577–1640),
The Anatomy of Melancholy

The Inner Compass

Some 40 per cent of the world's birds migrate. They do so for a variety of reasons, such as escaping extreme weather conditions, finding fresh food supplies or somewhere safe to moult, and to breed. Yet how they find their way remains something of a mystery.

It's been shown that birds can use landmarks such as coastlines, roads and valleys to orientate themselves. In daytime, the position of the Sun appears to guide them, whereas nocturnal migrant birds use the Moon and stars. There's also evidence that birds possess some sort of inner compass that can detect the Earth's magnetic field, helping them locate true north.

Interestingly, this compass isn't unique to birds – it has been detected in many other animals, from snails and frogs to lobsters and mammals. However, there's some debate about the nature of the compass, with one group of scientists saying it's formed by the protein cryptochrome, while another claims it's created from traces of the mineral magnetite – both of which are found in human beings.

Why not try a little experiment yourself? Get hold of a compass and, without glancing at it, point it in the direction you instinctively feel is true north. Now check the compass to see how close you are. Over the course of the next few weeks, repeat this exercise in a variety of places and at different times of day, keeping a record of the results. What are your findings?

Birds of Prey

How could I ever forget the rapt expression in those eyes? I will always cherish my memories of Spike, but it's highly unlikely he'll remember me. Spike was a little owl I met briefly at a birds of prey centre, where visitors were allowed to handle the owls, falcons and hawks under supervision. The falconer had hand-reared many of them and clearly loved them with a passion. (All in all, it was a much more successful visit than one to an equivalent centre abroad, where the eagle flew off, leaving his handler flapping about desperately, followed by his fellow falconer treating us to the close-up spectacle of a vulture biting the head off a chick.)

You can see the wild in the eyes of a bird of prey. While tame birds can be coaxed with titbits, they aren't particularly biddable by nature – yet they are beautiful to watch. In the lanes where I live, sparrowhawks swoop suddenly out of hedgerows and buzzards perch atop telegraph poles. Kestrels hover next to main roads and peregrines hunt along clifftops on the coast.

The world's fastest creature, the peregrine appears to be making a comeback in Britain's cities, nesting in cathedrals and roosting high up on ledges, including at London's Tate Modern. They enjoy something of an urban celebrity status, with many sites installing live webcams during the spring breeding season.

Discover more about the raptors where you live – what they are and where they can be found. When you see a bird of prey soaring high, what is your instinctive reaction?

FEATHER

Lark or Owl?

One winter's evening, I was walking through central London when I heard a blackbird singing its heart out from the corner of a building. It was lovely to hear but slightly disconcerting – as if the building's bright lights had deceived the bird into thinking it was still daytime.

Like birds and other animals, human beings are governed by their internal circadian clocks, which respond to light and dark and influence our sleeping and waking patterns. However, there's mounting evidence to suggest our use of modern technology and electric light is disrupting these rhythms. A study by researchers at the University of Colorado focused on a small group of campers who weren't allowed to use electronic gadgets, and discovered that after only a week the differences between the early and late risers – the so-called larks and owls – had lessened as all became more attuned to the natural light–dark cycle of the day. So it would seem that one way to reset your body clock to a more natural pace is to go gadget-free camping.

But you don't have to spend time under canvas. Experiment for a week by switching off all your electronic screens in the evenings and see if this makes a difference to the quality of your sleep. In the mornings, open the curtains as soon as you wake and spend as much time as you can in daylight. Listen to your body's instincts and see what happens next.

Eavesdropping on Skylarks

When you hear a skylark sing, it seems incredible that such a melodious sound could come from a little, brown, inconspicuous bird. Skylarks prefer open countryside to nest in and I've heard them trilling above wheat fields as well as over sand dunes. While they can be hard to spot on the ground, should you hear one, look up and search for a tiny dot of a bird suspended in the sky as if by song.

While worldwide there's no immediate cause for concern, changing farming practices mean that in recent years there has been a sharp decline in the numbers of skylarks in Europe. Although various schemes are in hand to help encourage agricultural biodiversity, it seems there's still work to be done to improve the fortunes of this small songster and others like it.

It's impossible to imagine how much we would be losing if our skies were to fall silent. Let's treasure the skylark and the sounds of spring while we still can.

—— ∞ ——

'Higher still and higher
From the earth thou springest
Like a cloud of fire ..'

PERCY BYSSHE SHELLEY (1792–1822),
'To a Skylark'

Pellet Power

Pellets are formed from the regurgitated remains of a bird's food: indigestible bits like seed husks, fur, bones and insect casings. While birds such as kestrels, jackdaws and gulls produce pellets, owl pellets are among the most interesting to study.

To find a pellet, look for a roosting site, taking great care not to disturb any birds (in the UK, it's illegal to disturb nesting barn owls). Then search the ground and ledges underneath. A barn owl pellet might be between 3 cm and 7 cm long (1–3 in), smooth, rounded and black when fresh; it shouldn't smell or be as long and pointy as fox scat. All the same, it's a good idea to wash your hands carefully or wear disposable gloves when handling pellets.

To discover what an owl has been eating, dissect the dry pellet or soak it first in water with a few drops of disinfectant to loosen it up. Using tweezers and wooden toothpicks, tease the pellet apart. The basic material is known as the matrix and might well be fur or the remains of feathers. Any white grubs are most likely the larvae of clothes moths (a good reason not to store pellets indoors, or to keep them in a sealed container if you do).

Look for the dainty bones of mice, voles and shrews – clues to where the bird has been hunting.

Once you've laid out the contents, you could glue the material to a card, along with a note of when and where the pellet was found. Then return to the site at different times of the year to discover whether the owl's diet changes. You might get to know all about its dining habits without even meeting it – the avian equivalent of all those food photos on Instagram.

—— ∞ ——

'All of the night was quite barred out except
An owl's cry, a most melancholy cry . . .'

EDWARD THOMAS (1878–1917), 'The Owl'

Fur

remember being outraged when, at the age of four or five, I learned that human beings were animals too. I'm not exactly sure what I'd thought we were – angels without wings perhaps. (Plenty of scope for disillusionment there.) Of course, as we go about our busy lives in built-up surroundings, brushing our teeth, combing our hair, it's all too easy to forget we're as much a part of the natural world as every other creature in it.

Get to know your animal neighbours by looking for signs of their presence – from tracks in the earth to burrows and nibbled tree bark or cracked nuts – and discover how to make life better for them. Be wild, be free, be at one with your extended family.

— ∞ —

'An animal's eyes have the power to speak a great language.'

MARTIN BUBER (1878–1965), *I and Thou*

Train Spotting

Many years ago, I knew a wonderful woman called Patrinella Cooper, who came from a long line of gypsy folk. She had an insatiable curiosity about life, and I remember her telling me how much she enjoyed travelling by train; there was always so much to see through the windows, she said, she never had time to read.

Her comment has stayed with me because, like so many of us, when I'm a train passenger I'm tempted to bury my head in a good book or check my phone for messages. Now, however, I make a conscious effort to look up and out at the passing landscape. Wherever wildlife has become used to a railway in its midst, you will very likely have the chance to see it getting on with daily life with no concern for a train's brief, rattling intrusion.

A friend once told me she'd never seen a hare in the wild, yet I often spot them when I'm on the train. Likewise, it's easy to sight birds of prey and deer. I've even seen a family of fox cubs cavorting in the sidings outside Waterloo Station in central London (perhaps not welcomed by the station staff, but fun to watch while the train sat waiting for a platform to become free).

Next time you're a passenger, take a moment to look out at the world flashing by. Perhaps set yourself a challenge and start your own train-spotting list, adding to it with each journey – jotting down any birds, animals and landscape features you notice.

Wild Visitors

Last summer, our garden was visited by a large badger. How do I know? Because the badger decided to mark its territory with a generous splattering of badger poo. It wasn't nice; it wasn't pretty; it was full of half-digested berries.

The joys of animal scat aside, there are other ways to tell whether a wild animal has been in the area. You might spot tracks, for instance – of which more later. Other tell-tale signs include tufts of fur snagged in fencing, sometimes left by deer or foxes, and obvious animal trails where the grass has been flattened and a small path worn into the undergrowth. (These are often created in fields by my friend the badger.)

Grazing and browsing marks are other clues. Hares and rabbits snip off leaves with their sharp incisors, while deer will shred vegetation. Song thrushes leave behind a pile of broken snail shells after dining, having smashed them open on a hard surface such as a rock or step.

In short, animals don't tend to go to much trouble to cover their tracks, so if you start to look deliberately for clues you might well be rewarded. When you're next out and about, keep your wits about you and note down any signs that you see, no matter where you are.

Invite the Neighbours to Dinner

If you aren't able to go out looking for wildlife, you could always invite the animals to come to you by creating your own tracking plot:

Clear a section of ground, leaving it free of debris.

Dig and turn over the top inch of soil. Then rake it to create a fine layer of earth where fresh footprints will be obvious. (If you don't want to dig up your lawn, simply fill a baking tray with damp sand, and pack the sand down to create a smooth surface.)

Place your bait in the middle of the plot. You could use a few berries, an apple core, crushed cat biscuits or a small helping of pet food (as long as it's not fish-based, as this doesn't sit well with hedgehogs).

Return the next day to discover the tracks of your visitors, and look them up in reference guides to get to know your wild neighbours.

Remember, though, the salutary tale of that messy badger visitor of mine; not all wild guests have particularly good manners. It might not be such a great idea to encourage larger mammals or rodents into your garden, so have a careful think about where you site your tracking plot.

Making Tracks

If you create your own tracking plot, you might well be rewarded with a fresh set of footprints from a nocturnal visitor. Elsewhere, animal tracks often appear on pathways, in trails of flattened vegetation and on muddy ground. Some of these footprints could be created by domestic animals, such as dogs and cats, especially around bins. Others, however, could be the mark of a wild visitor.

To get a sense of which animal might be in your neighbourhood, look for the number of toes or toe pads in the tracks, and note the size and depth of the print, and whether there are any claw marks.

I've roughly sketched some sets of animal tracks below (not all of which you might expect to find where you live, so please add to these with some sketches of your own).

(F) (H) Badger

Deer

(F) Otter (H)

(F) Rat (H)

Fox (F) (H)

Black Bear (F) (H)

An assortment of animal tracks – not drawn to scale (F = Front, H = Hind)

(H) (F) Hedgehog

Create an Animal Highway

As our surroundings become increasingly built up, it's important to keep wildlife corridors open. These link up different areas of habitat, allowing animals and insects to move around freely – vital for biodiversity. While you might not be able to encourage herds of migrating wildebeest past your sitting-room window, with a little effort you can help small mammals such as bats, shrews, voles and hedgehogs, as well as lizards, snakes, amphibians and insects to travel safely through your terrain. Moreover, creating a wildlife corridor is the perfect excuse for being a lazy gardener, as animals prefer groundcover such as long grass and shrubbery to wide-open spaces.

To create a wildlife corridor:

* If it's OK with your neighbour, create spaces in your fencing for wildlife to squeeze through. These can be about 15 cm wide by 12 cm high (6 × 5 in) for small mammals, or 8 cm by 6 cm (3 × 2½ in) for frogs and toads. Make sure any small pets of your own can't escape, though.
* Grow climbing plants such as honeysuckle and jasmine over fencing, walls and balconies to encourage insects and other animals to visit and cross over.
* Let some areas of your lawn grow longer.
* Plant shrubs for cover, and as a source of food.

F U R

* Provide drinking water in bird baths or in a bowl on the ground.
* Plant or put out pots of nectar-rich flowers such as lavender, Sweet William, bee balm and marjoram.

While you won't be thanked in person, the local wildlife will appreciate your efforts, and you will very likely see more of it.

—— ∞ ——

'No house should ever be on *a hill or* on *anything.*
It should be of *the hill. Belonging to it.'*
FRANK LLOYD WRIGHT (1867–1959),
Frank Lloyd Wright: An Autobiography

Badger Watching

In the UK, badgers have a reputation as divided as their black-and-white faces. Some people believe they should be culled to curb the spread of bovine TB, whereas others love them with a passion. If you'd like to find out more about them, try badger watching. Although it's easier to find a sett in the countryside, in recent years there has been an urban badger boom, with a 2014 survey finding they'd been spotted in a fifth of city gardens.

Badgers often build setts in hedgerows or in sloping woodland near fields where they can find earthworms. The large entrances to their setts are wider than high, and usually surrounded by piles of soft earth. Badgers *love* digging.

To go badger watching, dress in dark clothing that doesn't rustle and don't wear perfume or aftershave, as badgers have keen senses of hearing and smell. Arrive quietly at the sett an hour or so before twilight and hide yourself about 10 metres (11 yards) downwind from it. Bring binoculars if you have them and, if you wish, a torch covered with a red filter to shine close by. Then wait for the badgers to emerge. If you're lucky, they might oblige.

I once went badger watching with my husband and spent a good hour peering through the gloom at a tree stump. We gave up and turned to leave, only to find a badger merrily crashing through the undergrowth right behind us. It had probably been people watching.

Nutting

Scout around in the leaf litter beneath a hazel or oak tree in autumn, and you might come across a nut or an acorn with a tell-tale hole or crack it – a sure sign that a rodent has been feasting. Dormice and wood mice can bore beautiful little holes, turning hollowed nutshells into miniature bowls, whereas a squirrel will split a nut in half to empty it.

If you have access to a mature hazel tree or walnut tree, go nutting to create your own supplies. That's if you can get to the nuts before the local squirrels do. We once had a squirrel who not only raided the hazel tree in our garden, but stashed the nuts in our attic – thumping around at 5 a.m. every morning to retrieve them. While we feared for our wiring, we had to admire his perseverance . . .

Once you've successfully harvested your own haul, peel the green hull off any walnuts before storing them; if you press the skin, a ripe walnut hull will show the indentation. To sort good nuts from bad, put them in water and the rotten ones will float. Discard insect-infested nuts with

 holes in their shells and lay the remainder out to dry in a warm place for a couple of weeks. The drier they are, the easier they'll be to crack open. If left unshelled, hazelnuts and walnuts should last for several months. (Those squirrels aren't stupid.)

F U R

Rabbits and Hares

There are many myths and folktales about hares. Witches were once believed to be able to assume the shape of a hare and the animals were linked with that other shapeshifter, the Moon. Hares are fast, fluid and unpredictable.

If you spot a hare, you're unlikely to mistake it for a rabbit. Hares are much larger and lankier, with strong hind quarters and black tips on their ears. They don't live in burrows but create depressions in the ground known as forms, and can run at speeds of 40 mph. The adults are not very sociable animals, living alone or in pairs, and aren't easily tamed. It's thought the adjective 'hare-brained' comes from their skittish behaviour in captivity. Yes, hares have a definite edge about them.

If you find yourself travelling through flat arable land, keep a look-out and you might just spot a hare hunched low to the ground, or raised up on its back legs, scouring the horizon for danger or opportunity. Their very wildness invites us to examine our own attitudes to the natural world.

What does nature mean to you? Rabbit or hare? Friend or foe? To be tamed or to be worshipped? Perhaps all or none of these things . . .

Wild Indoors

Of course, you don't always have to venture outside if you want to see animals behaving wildly. Domestic animals such as dogs and cats share certain traits with their distant cousins and ancestors.

DNA evidence has shown that dogs split from wolves 40,000 years ago, yet they still exhibit some of the same behaviours. These include their sociability as pack animals, their vocal communications and even their body language – such as bowing when they want to play and adopting particular postures when they're being aggressive or submissive.

Although domestic cats are descended from the African wild cat, a study by Bronx Zoo has shown that they are actually like miniature lions, grooming to help them stay scent-free and hidden from prey animals, and rubbing up against things and scratching to mark their territory with their scent glands.

If you have a pet animal in your life and you want to honour its true nature, try to show a little respect for the beast within . . .

—— ∞ ——

'Society tames the wolf into a dog. And man is the most domesticated animal of all.'
FRIEDRICH NIETZSCHE (1844–1900),
Thus Spoke Zarathustra

FUR

How to Catch a Mouse

I have shared my home with a number of cats over the years. While they aren't everyone's favourite animal, if you've ever lived in a tiny cottage with a major rodent problem, you might come round to appreciating them. The cat currently in my life is, thankfully, not a very good hunter, but that doesn't stop him trying to give me lessons. He once brought in healthy mice three days in a row and released them for me to play with. And I was nowhere near as grateful as he expected. I did, however, turn out to be the better mouser.

If you have a mouse loose about the house, find a deep, dark boot. (As mice tend to pee a lot, you might prefer to use a boot belonging to somebody else.) Now corner the mouse as best you can, while offering the boot as a potential bolt hole. With a bit of persuading, the mouse will most likely run into it. At which point, tip the boot up with the mouse safely inside and take it outdoors where it can be released into the wild. If you like, sing 'Born Free' as the mouse scampers off.

Some friends once set free a mouse that had been caught in a humane trap. When they released it onto the grass the mouse took one look at the big wide world . . . and crawled back inside the box.

Well Groomed

When is fur not fur? When it's on a human and called hair. Hair and fur are both made of the protein keratin and go through growth cycles that consist of three distinct phases, at the end of which the hair or fur finally falls out – and the cycle begins all over again.

In human beings, the growth cycle typically lasts a lot longer than it does for animals. Where a dog or cat might seem to be shedding fur all over the carpet every day of the week, human scalp hair can keep on growing for up to seven years, while body hair might grow for a few months.

If, however, you're envious of your pet's silky coat and would like to return your hair to a more natural state, you could try the 'no-poo' method. A friend of mine has done it and her hair has never looked better. It means giving up shampoos and conditioners, and just washing your hair in warm water. If you like, you can occasionally use a mix of water and baking soda or diluted apple cider vinegar too.

Apparently the first few weeks are the worst as the hair will continue to overproduce sebum, a natural oil, resulting in greasy locks that you might want to hide away with a scarf or hat – until you finally emerge in your crowning glory.

The Art of Camouflage

For many animals, their fur and skin act as camouflage, enabling them to blur their silhouettes and blend into their surroundings so they can hide from predators or hunt successfully.

There are various types of camouflage, such as the concealing colouration used by Arctic animals like the polar bear, whose white fur helps it merge into snowy landscapes. Other animals such as leopards and tigers use disruptive camouflage – their spots, patterns and stripes break up their outlines, making them harder to see. Creatures such as stick insects use out-and-out disguise, whereas others use mimicry: the stripes of the stingless hoverfly, for example, make it resemble a bee.

Start to train your eye, looking beyond what immediately presents itself to you and uncover the layers of your surroundings so that you can spot animals hiding in plain sight. Take, for instance, that mound on the grass: is it a rock or a rabbit? Might a movement in the shadows be a deer, or a tabby cat resting in the shade? On a smaller scale, examine the underside of leaves to see what might be doing its best to remain hidden, and turn over rocks. Capture examples of everyday camouflage with notes and sketches in your journal.

I once came across a fox who sat completely still behind a clump of dock in the middle of a field. He clearly thought he was perfectly hidden among the dock's reddish leaves – apart from the fact that his ears stuck out on either side.

Cows Together

The saying goes that when cows lie down, rain is on the way – and perhaps there's a grain of truth in this. While cows seek shelter during a downpour, they often do seem to lie down before rain. But maybe that's just because we get a lot of wet weather in this part of the world. There could be other reasons for their behaviour; perhaps they're simply tired, hanging out chewing the cud or they don't need to stand up to cool down.

Cows can be unpredictable with people they don't know, so I'm wary of them when out walking, and stay out of fields with calves and their protective mothers or bulls, even if there's a public right of way. However, it can be interesting to watch cows among themselves – how, for instance, some stand on the outside of the herd as if taking turns to guard it. Each herd has its own hierarchy, and recent research suggests cows make individual friends. I've come across them peacefully grooming each other, so this doesn't seem surprising. Yet I'm intrigued by the notion of friendship among animals. If there's friendship, surely there must be altruism, empathy and kindness too?

When you next get the opportunity, spend some time watching a group of animals interact with each other. What do you discover?

Heaven Scent

Compared with many mammals, human beings appear to have a poor sense of smell. Bears have one of the most acute senses when it comes to sniffing out food and potential mates, and even cows can pick up scents five or six miles away. So what about us then?

Well, smell might mean more to us than we suppose. Research suggests that human beings could have unique 'odourtypes' – the olfactory equivalent of a fingerprint. Moreover, our sense of smell is key to unlocking taste and memories, and there are some super-smellers among us who are able to detect the onset of conditions such as Parkinson's disease before other symptoms are apparent. While a dog's sense of smell might be 10,000 to 100,000 times more acute than a human being's, ours is still not to be sniffed at. In fact, let's celebrate it.

To make a simple perfume, pick fragrant flowers such as lavender, jasmine, orange blossoms (if available), roses and honeysuckle. Remove stems and greenery before bundling the fresh flowers in muslin or cheesecloth and placing them in a bowl of water. Steep for 24 hours before removing the bundle and squeezing out any excess liquid into the bowl. Then simmer the liquid till there's only a spoonful or two left. Pour this into a clean container, and you're done.

Another method, requiring more patience, is to cram scented flowers into a jar of unflavoured gin or vodka. Seal and keep for six months before straining the liquid and bottling. (You can use the dried petals afterwards as potpourri.) Try different combinations of flowers to find the fragrance you like best.

— ∞ —

*'Nothing is more memorable than a smell. One scent can
be unexpected, momentary and fleeting, yet conjure up
a childhood summer beside a lake in the mountains; another,
a moonlit beach; a third, a family dinner of pot roast and sweet
potatoes during a myrtle-mad August in a Midwestern town.'*

DIANE ACKERMAN (1948–),
A Natural History of the Senses

FUR

Burrowing Down

Many animals besides badgers and rabbits live in burrows and holes. The size of the entrance is usually a good clue to the occupier (although you might discover a weasel nesting in an old vole burrow or even occasionally find rabbits, foxes and rats sharing a badger's sett). While dinosaur burrows have been found in south-eastern Australia and the American state of Montana, today the largest burrowing animal is probably the bear, which makes dens in which to hibernate and rear its cubs.

A burrow might be an animal's home, a nursery, a place of safety or even a larder. If you come across one, take care not to upset the residents while you make a note of where it is, how wide the entrance is and whether there are any give-away smells. Look for signs such as tracks and scat, as well as tufts of fur, bits of bedding, cropped vegetation or traces of food. If you have a camera with you, take a photo or two to help build up the picture.

And enjoy the fact that here is the home of a wild animal, going about its life freely.

'Lying in my heap of earth I can naturally dream of all sorts of things.'

FRANZ KAFKA (1883–1924), 'The Burrow'

Mole in a Hole

Unwelcome in most gardens because of the damage molehills do to neat lawns, moles are industrious animals rarely seen above ground. Their elaborate tunnel systems include packed larders and chambers lined with grass for nests. They can paralyse prey such as earthworms with toxins in their saliva, and have adapted to subterranean life in extraordinary ways, with extra thumbs for digging and the ability to rebreathe their own expired air through their blood's 'super' haemoglobin. Their unique velvety fur has no direction to the nap, allowing them to move backwards without ruffling themselves up.

While a mole's eyesight is poor – some even have skin over their eyes – moles can see, and their eyes help regulate their body clocks. They also possess the ability to smell in stereo and their nose is covered with tiny touch receptors. In a way, a mole's nose acts a little like fingers, allowing them to feel their way and respond to their environment through touch.

Despite often being ignored, touch influences nearly every aspect of our own lives too – from gauging textures and temperatures, to experiencing pleasure and pain. Touch can be therapeutic and formative, an essential part of our interactions with the world. To give touch its due, spend a day or two focusing on this sense and note down your findings. Look at the ways in which animals, insects, people and even plants use touch. How, for example, does touch help you appreciate your surroundings and shape the ways in which you respond?

Pop! Goes the Weasel

Every now and then when I'm in the car, a streak of russet will bolt across the road ahead: a weasel or stoat rushing to the other side. I've occasionally come across one hunting in the fields, making little piles of dead shrews.

While it can be tricky to tell the difference between stoats and weasels, stoats are slightly bigger with creamier fur on their undersides and black tips to their tails, while a weasel's tail is brown and its underside is white.

Mustelids such as weasels, stoats and martens are pretty creatures – and ruthless killers. They have an unusual tactic at their disposal: a war dance. When approaching prey such as rabbits, weasels and stoats might suddenly start hopping, twisting and scampering about, edging ever closer. Their wild behaviour seems to confuse or even hypnotise their quarry, until they're close enough to dispatch it with a sharp bite to the nape of the neck.

There's a theory that their death dance might be triggered by the presence of parasites in their nasal sinuses; be that as it may, it's a hunting technique that works. With their weasel ways, they demonstrate the dangers of enchantment by distraction and of being dazzled

FUR

by displays. And yet there's a grim pleasure in watching them perform. It's easy to see why they have taken their place in fables and why we use terms such as 'weasel words'.

In your journal, take a moment to consider how an animal's natural behaviour might shed light upon our own, and explore zoomorphism as opposed to anthropomorphism.

— ∞ —

'With bats, weasels, worms – I rejoice in the kinship.
Even the caterpillar I can love, and the various vermin.'

THEODORE ROETHKE (1908–1963), 'Slug'

Bats

Stepping outside on a warm summer's evening at dusk, I'm often rewarded with the sight of bats flittering through the air, catching insects on the wing. The only mammals to fly, bats live in a wide variety of habitats, from woodlands and caves to city centres and the roof spaces of modern houses.

In built-up areas, gardens are important hunting grounds for them. To encourage bats into yours, let wild grasses, shrubs, herbs and night-scented flowers grow, and perhaps build a small pond. This will attract moths and other insects for them to feed on, and it might enhance your own surroundings, as bat-friendly flowers include beauties such as echinacea, mallow, night-scented stock, English marigold and ox-eye daisy. Keep your outdoor lighting to a minimum and shut cats indoors at night. Then, once bats come a-calling, sit back and enjoy their aerial antics.

If you don't have a garden, go bat spotting in a park or field near trees and hedgerows, which bats use to help them navigate, or contact your local bat spotting group, who might have bat detector equipment that will enable you to listen to bats flying and hunting using echolocation.

In spite of their starring roles in horror films and slightly grumpy expressions, bats make for considerate neighbours by keeping insect numbers down and acting as pollinators and seed dispersers for plants; much more akin to the Caped Crusader than Dracula.

Night Shift

If, on a dark winter's night, you hear an unearthly shriek, try to remain calm. It might sound like murder but it's probably only the cry of a vixen, looking for love. During the brief mating season and when defending their territories, foxes can shriek and scream like a bag of fighting cats.

The night holds other strange noises. A rasping bark like a dog with a sore throat could well be the call of a deer, while badgers also bark and yelp. A single screech is possibly the cry of a barn owl, and birds such as starlings, redwings and thrushes migrate under the cover of darkness, so might be heard as they fly overhead.

Discover the sounds of the night yourself. Sit at an open window or head out into the dark. If the latter, stay safe: let someone know where you're going or go with a friend, wrap up warm, and take a torch and phone with you. Don't trespass but do wander, keeping your senses alert.

Stand silently and listen to the night unfolding around you.

— ∞ —

'The day has eyes, the night has ears.'

Proverb

In Conclusion – A Beginning...

Working on this book has been a joy, reawakening memories and reminding me of the incredible diversity of life – animals, plants, the changing seasons, sky and elements – that surrounds us wherever we are. It has refreshed my appreciation of the land that I live in and brought to mind the freedoms I took for granted when I was growing up. I belong to a generation who were routinely expected to entertain themselves when young, which usually meant getting grubby somewhere outdoors, sharing discoveries, trying things out and taking risks. We would suck nectar from dead-nettle flowers, build camps on wasteland, scrabble through hedgerows and hold solemn funerals for dead shrews. As long as we were back home in time for tea, nobody minded too much where we disappeared off to.

While the world might have changed, I believe that, whatever our age and wherever we live, we still need that hands-on connection with nature. A connection with nature isn't just about good parenting and something fun to do with the kids; it's rooted in a deep-seated instinct and is a fundamental part of who we are, answering one of our basic needs as human beings.

Academic research is continuing to explore the relationship between spending time in a healthy natural environment and well-being, so soon we may have an even deeper understanding of the many ways in which being in nature benefits us physically and emotionally. And yet in some respects it seems ironic that we should need to formalise our relationship with nature at all. Our instincts draw us to blue and green spaces, so rather than waiting to be told officially that it's good for us, we might just need to start listening to ourselves and get out more when we can.

Nature isn't all buttercups and butterflies, but it's incredibly diverse and thought-provoking – and you are part of it too, with a role to play in the future of this beautifully complex planet. My hope is that the suggestions and snippets of information in these pages will inspire you to put this book down, or to cram it in a backpack, and go out to rediscover nature for yourself. By spending time in the natural world, perhaps you will even uncover unexplored aspects of your own true nature: hidden talents maybe, untapped feelings, calm, contentment and insights into who you are and your place in the greater scheme of things.

Enjoy this wild adventure, wherever it takes you next.

—— ∞ ——

'May the road rise up to meet you.
May the wind be always at your back.
May the sun shine warm upon your face,
The rains fall soft upon your fields and until we meet again,
May God hold you in the palm of His hand.'

Gaelic blessing

IN CONCLUSION

Notes

The following blank pages are for you to fill with your own notes, thoughts, observations, sketches, doodles, and bits and pieces stuck in with glue or sticky tape – in fact, whatever you like. Once these pages have filled up, feel free to let your notes spill out into the rest of the book . . .

NOTES

NOTES

Further Reading

Mike Abbott, *Green Woodwork*, Guild of Master Craftsman, 1989

Daniel Allen, *The Nature Magpie*, Icon Books, 2013

Margaret Baker, *Discovering the Folklore of Plants*, Shire Classics, 2011

Jack Cooke, *The Tree Climber's Guide*, HarperCollins, 2016

Michael Davidson (ed.), *Field Guide to the Birds of Britain*, Reader's Digest, 1994

Paul Evans, *Field Notes from the Edge*, Rider Books, 2015

Tristan Gooley, *The Natural Navigator*, Ebury Publishing, 2010

Melissa Harrison, *Rain*, Faber & Faber, 2016

Matt Merritt, *A Sky Full of Birds*, Rider Books, 2016

Thomas Pakenham, *Meetings with Remarkable Trees*, Weidenfeld & Nicolson, 1996

Kevin Parr, *Rivers Run*, Rider Books, 2016

J. R. Press, D. A. Sutton and B. R. Tebbs, *Field Guide to the Wild Flowers of Britain*, Reader's Digest, 1982

John Seymour, *The Forgotten Arts & Crafts*, Dorling Kindersley, 2001

Peter Tate, *Flights of Fancy*, Arrow Books, 2009

Colin Tudge, *The Secret Life of Trees*, Penguin Books, 2006

Acknowledgements

Every book is a collaboration. Working on this one has made me more aware than ever of how lucky I am to enjoy the guidance and friendship of some special people. For their support along the way, I would particularly like to thank the following:

Grace Cheetham, for the opportunity to write this book, and for her gentle and wise counsel and encouragement at every step – thank you. Thanks too to Micaela Alcaino, Fionnula Barrett, Mark Bolland, Terence Caven, Simon Gerratt, Jasmine Gordon and their colleagues at HarperCollins for all their hard work and creativity in the face of some serious deadlines.

Bill Anderson, Jenny Benjamin, Helen Chamberlain, Clare Chandler, Claire Mason and Peter Vince, for generous suggestions and insights.

Katrin Maclean, Stella Maden, Ashley Morgan, Helen Pisano, Jane Pizzey, Kath Rhodes and Andrew Wille, for many kindnesses and valuable advice.

The Belfrage and Lascelles clans, for being there.

Matt Belfrage, for being him.

About the Author

Sue Belfrage lives in a cottage in rural Somerset with her furniture-maker husband and pet animals. Born in Liverpool, she lived in Sweden for a while as a child, where she discovered a love of nature before moving back to the English countryside. Today, she is a writer and artist who draws inspiration from the land around her.